Aparna Sen

Aparna Sen

A Life in Cinema

Devapriya Sanyal

RUPA

Published by
Rupa Publications India Pvt. Ltd 2025
161-B/4, Gulmohar House,
Yusuf Sarai Community Centre,
New Delhi 110049

Sales centres:
Bengaluru Chennai
Hyderabad Kolkata Mumbai

The views and opinions expressed in this book are the author's own and the facts are as reported by her; these have been verified to the extent possible, and the publishers are not in any way liable for the same.

P-ISBN: 978-93-7003-865-3
E-ISBN: 978-93-7003-771-7

First impression 2025

10 9 8 7 6 5 4 3 2 1

Printed in India

For

Professor Harish Narang, who guided me through the labyrinth of words, who taught me the value of critical thinking, and the power of the pen.

Contents

Introduction
The World of Aparna Sen

Cinema has always been an integral part of Bengal, alongside theatre and politics. Some of the most celebrated practitioners of these arts hail from Bengal. While Bengali cinema consistently made its mark nationally, it was Satyajit Ray's *Pather Panchali* (1955) that brought it global recognition. Following in Ray's footsteps, Aparna Sen carved out a distinct space for herself as a three-time National Award-winning director with a career spanning over four decades. Known for her nuanced and sensitive storytelling, Sen has contributed significantly to both Bengali and Indian cinema, earning accolades nationally and internationally. While she began her cinematic journey as an actor, it is her work as a director that truly defines her legacy.

This legacy ties into broader questions about gender and aesthetics in cinema. In 1976, Silvia Bovenschen asked, 'Is there a feminine aesthetic?' She suggested that while aesthetic awareness and sensory perception might differ along the lines of gender, artistic production itself might not necessarily exhibit these differences. In India, the cinematic representation of women has long grappled with breaking away from stereotypical binaries—virgin versus vamp, femme fatale versus angel in the house. Despite efforts to present more realistic portrayals of women in films like *Aandhi* (1975), *Bhumika: The Role* (1977), and *Arth* (1982), such portrayals often remained overshadowed by entrenched societal attitudes. Against this backdrop, women directors like Aparna Sen stand out for challenging these norms. Alongside contemporaries like Kalpana Lajmi and Sai Paranjpye, Aparna Sen pushed the boundaries of cinematic narratives, offering stories that resist simplistic readings—placing women at the centre of complex, multidimensional narratives.

Beginnings

In several of her interviews, Sen proudly reminisces about the fact that she was brought up on a diet of films that were completely different from the kind she mostly acted in. In fact, she states that at home, there was strict proscription on watching mainstream Bengali or Hindi cinema. She says that her father had also promised her a film worth watching in Satyajit Ray's *Pather Panchali*, which she eagerly awaited. Her movie-watching, instead, included world cinema, which the Calcutta Film Society—founded by her father Chidananda Dasgupta and Satyajit Ray—showcased. These films which were scarcely known to the average Bengali moviegoer of those times brought together a gamut of Calcutta intellectuals, many of whom became filmmakers later on, one of them being Harisadhan Dasgupta, not to mention Ray and Chidananda Dasgupta himself.

At one point, the Film Society meetings were often held

in a room in Dasgupta's house, during which the cinema of Sergei Eisenstein, Carl Theodor Dreyer, Vsevolod Pudovkin, Robert Flaherty, John Grierson, Marcel Carné, Julien Duvivier, Akira Kurosawa and such others was animatedly discussed; she was privy to these discussions. As she grew up, besides world cinema, Sen was exposed to a wide range of world literature: while on the one hand she was introduced to Bengali classics, namely Bankim Chandra Chatterjee and Rabindranath Tagore, along with other more contemporary Bengali writers, she also voraciously read English and European classics on the other.

A lively cultural environment prevailed in the home Sen and her sisters grew up in. Apart from future filmmakers, well-known writers, among them Kamal Kumar Majumdar, Buddhadeva Bose, Jibanananda Das (who was also Sen's mother's first cousin) and other stalwarts, frequented the Dasgupta household and engaged in highly productive *addas* to which the children had unrestricted access. Sen recalls with a sense of gratitude that these addas, in which literature, cinema, theatre, world politics and other burning issues of the times were conferred on, were most influential in shaping her own worldview.

As an Actor

In 1961, exactly 20 years prior to her directorial debut with *36 Chowringhee Lane*, the world was introduced to Aparna Sen, née Dasgupta, the daughter of eminent film critic Chidananda Dasgupta, as the young Mrinmoyee of 'Samapti', a part of Satyajit Ray's *Teen Kanya* (1961). Sen says that this was in keeping with the fact that she had always wanted to be an actor, and her parents indulged her dreams and even promised to send her abroad to the Royal Academy of Dramatic Art (RADA) in London.

In 1969, she returned in a brief role in Ray's cinema to play Samit Bhanja's love interest in *Aranyer Din Ratri*. While her career as an actor was not exactly stellar to begin with, very soon she went on to become one of the most popular actresses of Bengali cinema. Her pairing with some of the top male stars of the industry, such as Uttam Kumar and Soumitra Chatterjee, lent a certain sheen and appeal to her films and made her an extremely popular star in turn. *Baksa Badal* (1970) and *Jay Jayanti* (1971) continue to remain some of her most popular films. Even as an actress, she played the roles of educated, working and empowered women, so it really does not come as a surprise that the women in the cinema which she would go on to create would be superior creatures compared to the men therein.

While she does not like to talk about her career as an actress, it is worthwhile to probe her career as one. Most of the earlier films she acted in—being products of the mainstream Tollygunge-based Bengali film industry—fetched stardom and an iconic status for her, which have still not waned. Aparna Sen is not only one of a very small group of female actors-turned-directors (others include Sai Paranjpye, Hema Malini, Pooja Bhatt, Nandita Das and Revathi), but also the best known of them. She is recognized not only for her direction and acting, but also as a cultural and sociopolitical commentator. She was also the editor of the immensely popular Bengali magazine called *Sananda* from 1986 to 2005, when Madhumita Chattopadhyay took over as the editor-in-chief. But more about that later.

Like Sharmila Tagore who made her cinematic debut

with Ray, Aparna Sen too straddled both worlds—she appeared in parallel or art films while having a remarkable presence in the 'commercial' genre of Bengali cinema in which she was often cast opposite the matinee idol Uttam Kumar. However, as Sen repeatedly expresses with displeasure, she was never happy acting in commercial films, and given her exposure to world cinema and other avant-garde art forms, she was extremely critical of such films with clichéd plots, a lack of innovation in form and content, and melodramatic acting. In fact, her condescension towards the commercial film earned her the tag 'snob' within the film industry.

The first draft of her debut film as a director, *36 Chowringhee Lane* (1981), as Sen likes to recount, came into being in the make-up room of a Bombay studio, as she waited to be called for the next shot of one of those many commercial films she could not intellectually connect to: 'I began writing a short story out of exasperation. I asked myself whether I should continue to act in such films in which I did not believe.' Sen did not stop acting in these films, though. For that earned her a livelihood. But she was creatively inclined to art-house cinema which, however, did not have as many viewers.

In the 1960s and 1970s, she acted in films as aesthetically diverse as *Akash Kusum* (1965) directed by Mrinal Sen, and Satyajit Ray's *Aranyer Din Ratri*, at the same time as a commercially successful film such as *Jay Jayanti* (1971) with the reigning superstar of the day, Uttam Kumar, as well as others such as *Mem Saheb* (1972), *Basanta Bilap* (1973), *Rater Rajanigandha* (1973), *Chhutir Phande* (1974) and *Proxy* (1977), and several others that soon followed. And in all of them, Aparna Sen was portrayed as a sophisticated, sometimes rather westernized, if not too radical, woman. In recent years, she has become extremely selective about acting in films. If she happens to appear in one at all, it is usually in a meaningful role, central to the plot. Her last film was the Suman Ghosh-directed *Basu Paribar* (loosely based on James Joyce's 'The Dead') in 2019, where she played Soumitra Chatterjee's wife.

In her later films, Sen—who evolved with changing times—continued to play emancipated urban characters, often breaking stereotypes and emerging iconic in her dignified rebellion against patriarchal norms. One such film was Rituparno Ghosh's *Unishe April* (1994), which dramatized a widowed dancer's difficult relationship with her daughter, who failed to empathize with her mother's uncompromising pursuit of her career and apparent neglect of her household. In Aniruddha Roy Chowdhury's 2009 film *Antaheen*, she played the role of a successful journalist-cum-photographer who prioritized her career over family and lost it. In Srijit Mukherji's 2018 film *Ek Je Chhilo Raja*, she played the role of the prosecution lawyer who came across as an independent and fiery individual.

The Woman, the Movies

Aparna Sen possesses a unique grace, beauty and charm that remain striking even in her seventies. In her films, her beauty often takes a backseat to her commanding feminine presence. She comes across as spontaneous, thoughtful and profoundly intelligent. Over time, she seems to have come to embody the strong, determined and unconventional characters she has portrayed onscreen—qualities that now define her work as a director and make her stand out.

Much like her mentor Satyajit Ray, Sen's films show a deep and abiding faith in human goodness. And in all her films, one can easily notice the enduring influence of Satyajit Ray, as one finds intertextual hints that inevitably remind one of the master craftsman.

All her films offer several readings, and are not reducible to any fixed meaning. Each of her films expresses a woman's personal experience imbued with a political charge. The dominant themes of her oeuvre include loneliness, a search for meaning, sometimes love, most often identity. Some of her films depict immense beauty, pain and solitude. Other themes include art, the idea of freedom, the dynamics of personal relationships—especially those of women with their immediate surroundings—and questions of sexuality which inform her cinema. Even though her films are deeply rooted in the local Bengali culture, they are nonetheless universal in execution. Her cinema carries within itself her familiarity with a cultural milieu in which she matured as an artist, and at the same time, displays an intense awareness of international cinema, art and literature.

There is a long-standing debate in cinema studies surrounding the role of a director in terms of their input as an auteur in the filmmaking process. Much like Satyajit Ray who took charge of all the components of filmmaking, Aparna Sen, too, has a say in everything, from scriptwriting and music composition to the final mounting of the film.

Aparna Sen's films reflect a stark realism, and have occasioned provocative and robust discussions among the intelligentsia as well as her audience. Her films look at the dark edges of life that remain unexplored in other cinemas and are informed by deeply humanistic values, and at the same time, they are portraits of enduring relationships in a chaotic and violent world. Nevertheless, it is interesting to note that the context of each of her films is different, as are the content, the stylistic approaches, the music, cinematography and editing. Sen brings something intensely personal to each of her films, which successfully critique the limits of dominant cinema in terms of representing women. In her cinema, the women are successfully able to find a voice of their own.

Her Celluloid World

Sen started out at a time when women directors were few and far between; she took a tough stand by creating films that answered her need for a different kind of cinema. She was one of the key women directors to emerge in India in the early 1980s. Her first feature film was pathbreaking, and it not only set the tenor for other directors who were keen to follow in her footsteps, but also provided a template for other films that wanted to be different. Aparna Sen emerged as a radical filmmaker, challenging normative assumptions about women, sexualities and conventional moralities.

Sen's films are visually magnificent but in a subtle way. Her play is always on gender dynamics, and her focus is always on the inner workings of a woman's mind. Her understanding of the language of cinema makes the visuals powerful and compelling. Take, for instance, a film like *Mr. and Mrs. Iyer* (2002) with panoramic shots as exposition—visually beautiful shots accompanied by a haunting tune that stays long with you as the bus makes its way down to the valley. The various scenes promise you a sense of beauty and delight, but it is in the heart of nature that man will attempt desperate things—the

Jew will tell on the Muslim so that he is spared while the other is led to slaughter, and chaos will reign supreme as violence erupts all around. And amidst this, Meenakshi Iyer will suddenly discover her humanity and another world—that of love—with Jahangir Chowdhury aka Raja, a photographer.

In *36 Chowringhee Lane*, Sen looks at the almost lost community of Anglo-Indians through the eyes of her protagonist Ms Violet Stoneham; along with that, one gets glimpses of Calcutta in the 1980s. However, Sen's emphasis is on loneliness and the need for love which Miss Stoneham feels. Noted film scholar Wimal Dissanayake sees the film as a study of the patriarchal social system: 'The film portrays the plight of a lonely woman in a society that cares little for questions for female subjectivity and self-fulfillment.'[1]

In *Parama* (1985), Aparna Sen seeks an identity not only for her protagonist Parama, but also for all women in society. What constructs the self and the identity of a woman are the questions which Sen asks in this film. Although Parama discovers her inner self and desires through Rahul, a man, what is important is that she makes these choices on her own. Parama then is the story of a woman's awakening. Aparna makes Parama come back to her family after an affair, determined to live for herself, and continue to search for her own identity. The film was deemed controversial, opening a floodgate of protests back then. In spite of that, Sen braved on, and has, in film after

[1]Dissanayake, Wimal, 'Questions of Female Subjectivity and Patriarchy: a Reading of Three Indian Women Film Directors', *East-West Film Journal*, Vol. 3, No. 2, June 1989, pp. 74–90.

film, continued her quest for articulating an authentic woman's voice that seeks to transform society through art.

In *Yugant* (1995), Aparna explores, or rather, questions the institution of Indian marriage in a postmodern urban setting. The film is about the disintegration of a marriage threatened by environmental disaster and changing values. Her film *Sati* (1989) encapsulates perhaps the intrinsic yearning for companionship among human beings. The film explores the silent communion between a mute girl and a tree, while *Paromitar Ek Din* (2000) explores the rather unlikely but enduring friendship between Sanaka, the mother-in-law and a passionate woman with a zest for life, and her sensitive and affectionate daughter-in-law Paromita. Their relationship is ruptured when Paromita leaves the family to marry a second time, and Sanaka, deprived once again, dies of heartbreak and loneliness. Sanaka and Paromita draw upon each other's strengths to negotiate their relationships with various members of a conservative patriarchal family. The focus of the film then becomes the friendship between the two women or women's camaraderie, which is a rarity in Indian cinema.

The women in *15 Park Avenue* (2005), Dr Verma and Meethi, test social boundaries by attempting to claim their rightful positions and rights, not because they are feminists in the Anglo-American tradition, but because Sen actually lends her characters the knowledge and agency to rebel against their constricted circumstances. On the other hand, Sen's 2010 film *The Japanese Wife* (2010) is an improbable, (almost) surreal love story, and a different take on the world and women—a unique addition to her oeuvre. Based on a novel of the same name penned by Oxford-based author Kunal Basu, it tells the story of a village schoolteacher who marries his penpal in Japan, whose physical form he never sets eyes on, connecting exclusively through their letters. Of the film, Aparna says, 'I feel all human beings are lonely at some level and I like exploring a character to the point where I reach that loneliness.'[2]

To my mind, her film *Iti Mrinalini* (2011) is partly autobiographical in tone as it charts the journey of an acclaimed Bengali film actress from her youth until her demise. The film explores the psyche of Mrinalini, as issues of marginalization, identity, love and memories come to the fore through Aparna's deft handling of Mrinalini's life story. *Goynar Baksho* (2013) is an adaptation of a novella by the popular Bengali writer Shirshendu Mukhopadhyay, which looks at three generations of women and explores their sexuality and desires, as well as their resourcefulness. Aparna Sen enriches the film with her profound understanding of women's agency (or the lack of it) in the face of patriarchy.

Arshinagar (2015) is a musical adaptation of the Bard's *Romeo and Juliet*. Aparna says of the film, 'Looking back (and the producers along with a lot of people who loved the film) felt *Arshinagar* was a film that was before its time.'[3] The eminent political scientist Partha Chatterjee also celebrated the film in his article: 'Brilliantly innovative, Sen has combined the natural realism of the cinema with the staged dramatic narration of the theatre, to produce a form never seen in Bengali cinema before. What makes *Arshinagar* a landmark in Bengali cinema is the fact that formal innovation in commercial entertainment is always a risky business...everyone who wishes for a different future

---

[2]Interview with the author.
[3]Interview with the author.

for cinema in West Bengal will/should congratulate Sen for her remarkably courageous achievement in *Arshinagar*.'[4]

Influences

A central influence in Aparna Sen's life perhaps has been that of her father, the celebrated critic and filmmaker Chidananda Dasgupta, whose writings on cinema were not only seminal but also remain influential in the world of film criticism in India. One of her father's closest friends was Satyajit Ray, with whom Dasgupta would go on to found the Calcutta Film Society in 1947. Ray himself famously forged a new path in filmmaking and radicalized Bengali cinema's images, symbols and language. The trio of Satyajit Ray, Ritwik Ghatak and Mrinal Sen undoubtedly influenced Aparna's choice to become not only a filmmaker but also one with a distinct cinematic language. Her years as an actor no doubt helped hone her skills in directing films, making it easier for her to understand when an actor had problems with certain movements or lines. Says Sen: 'It also helped me in writing dialogue, by acting lines out in my head before I actually wrote anything down.'[5]

Of Ray's cinema, Chidananda Dasgupta wrote, '…neither in content nor in style did Ray's films owe anything at all to Bengali, indeed Indian, cinema traditions…'[6] Arguably, then, Ray ushered in another cinematic tradition that

---

[4]Chatterjee, Partha, 'A different future: Aparna Sen's innovative adaptation of Romeo and Juliet', *The Telegraph Online,* 13 December 2015, https://tinyurl.com/y6evfnn6. Accessed on 15 December 2022.

[5]Interview with the author.

[6]Dasgupta, Chidananda, *The Cinema of Satyajit Ray*, National Book Trust, New Delhi, 1994, p. 32.

combined the modern with the traditional, the global with the local, which Aparna undoubtedly drew upon. Aparna says, 'It is very difficult not to be influenced by Ray in the same way that writers were influenced by Tagore. At that time, he was like a huge banyan tree. We had come from the same kind of background—enlightened liberal Brahmo stock.'[7] Her unique cinematic medium—localized in high Bengali culture, but at the same time intelligible to a global audience—was perhaps constructed by following in the footsteps of her two mentors, the two Bengali giants Tagore and Ray.

In Aparna Sen's cinema, the women are categorized by specificities (almost granting them a real life) such as class positions and family backgrounds, almost always portraying various intimate interpersonal relationships. This can be seen through a close examination of the women in her various films—Miss Stoneham in *36 Chowringhee Lane*, Meenakshi Iyer in *Mr. and Mrs. Iyer*, the eponymous character in *Parama*, Meethi in *15 Park Avenue,* to name just a few.

Not being didactic, Sen's films do not offer forced happy closures for her women. Again, there are no binaries in terms of representation of women. The women are probed until their inner beings shine through.

At the time that Aparna was making her presence felt, Bengali commercial cinema was at an all-time low. Greatly influenced by the Bombay template which basically meant the 'angry young man' phenomenon, it came to imbue the same with a unique local feel.

In the 1980s and 1990s, there was a complete departure

---

[7]Sen, Aparna, 'Interview with Sandip Ray', *Aparna Sen Blog*, 13 July 2009, https://tinyurl.com/bdzk9vfj. Accessed on 15 December 2022.

from social reality into the realm of folk and fantasy. However, it was Aparna Sen and later Rituparno Ghosh who drew the middle class back to the theatres with their brand of cinema. With *Parama* and later the other films, Sen came to raise some important questions about gender, sexuality, marriage and motherhood, and what these terms meant to the middle class.

Aparna's cinema, though rooted in the Ray-Ghatak-Sen school and to a certain extent also influenced by parallel cinema, announced a phase that would come to be called 'Middle Cinema', which is distinct in form, style and intellectual complexity. While Aparna's films are realistic portrayals of social and political issues often played out in a domestic scenario, her difference from other directors is marked by her portrayal of women characters enacting their agency within a patriarchal Bengali society. It is precisely this which grants her films a certain universality, and in turn, they reach a wider audience, thus extending her regional identity to that of a national director. Her choice of stories, the art of narrating them, cinematic style, realism, simplicity, and the absence of flamboyance mark her cinema, and lend her oeuvre a certain distinction.

Several critics including Shoma Chatterji opine that like many women film directors (of which there were very few when Sen made her mark), Aparna Sen represents a feminine sensibility in the way she portrays women's negotiations with Indian patriarchy. Sen herself rejects the idea of her films being labelled feminist: 'I don't believe in any "ism" other than humanism...women's issues are to me a part and parcel of humanism itself—something that I believe in and try my best to live by.'[8]

In addition to her career as a filmmaker, Aparna Sen was also the editor of *Sananda*, one of the most influential women's magazines in Bengali launched in 1986 by the ABP Group. In the capacity of an editor, she became a cultural commentator through her various columns, and also played an active part, through the magazine's forum, in entering into dialogues with her readers on various issues such as communalism and sexuality rights, alongside home remedies and cooking tips. Being a socially conscientious critic who participated in several humanitarian and political causes, she has become a figure of trust and reliance for her many fans and detractors alike.

As early as 1989, Sen was a member of the jury at the 16th Moscow International Film Festival. In 2008, she was elected to the international jury of the Asia Pacific Screen Awards. In 2013, she headed the jury of the second Ladakh International Film Festival. Her films have also been a part of retrospectives at the National Theatre and the Institute of Contemporary Arts, London. She is also the third Indian since Satyajit Ray and Mrinal Sen to have won the NETPAC Jury Award at the Locarno Film Festival in 2002.

The Tenor of the Book

This book attempts to look at Aparna Sen's women as she weaves their stories on celluloid—how they journey from

---

[8]'"Feminism is part of humanism": Aparna Sen', *Dhaka Tribune*, 16 January 2018, https://tinyurl.com/27y3mrf2. Accessed on 17 December 2022.

being emotionally vulnerable creatures to claiming agency for themselves. Sen focuses her attention on the distinct sociocultural and economic contexts that inform, restrict and de-limit women's choices in various walks of life.

Apart from the introduction and the afterword, it is divided into seven chapters, five of which intend to show how Aparna Sen's cinema not only comes to enunciate new and often controversial themes, but how they also inscribe powerful meanings through a compelling and often innovative fashioning of varied discourses that she forges out of an Indian sensibility and a Western form of expression and resources. This book is thus a celebration of this and much more. It also attempts to decode her ideas, her story, and her life. For in the end, we are the stuff of stories that we are a part of, ones that we create and ones that others tell of us.

This work is a personal endeavour to put Aparna Sen in perspective within her industrial and cultural context. I study the films within her oeuvre that chart her evolution as a filmmaker, moving from exclusively gender-related concerns in her early films to political ones in her later work. In this, I have left out two films—*The Japanese Wife* and *Sonata* (2017)—from my analysis, which, in my opinion, do not represent the best of her oeuvre. In a way, the book celebrates the creative powers of Aparna Sen and chronicles the memories of those who have played their part in her cinema and her life.

Aparna Sen and the Representation of Women

The Case of Hindi Cinema

Since its very inception a hundred years ago, Indian cinema has seen various changes, evolving from mythology-based narratives to more recent blockbusters—technically improved, flashy, and focusing on a variety of themes—which are now the order of the day. While women in the film industry have always been an indispensable part of the movies, their representations have hardly undergone much change.

Examining the so-called progressive, women-centric films of the Hindi film industry seems to be a logical step in understanding the difference between prescriptive roles for women in Hindi cinema and the more individual-centric representations of women in Bengali art cinema, and more specifically, Aparna Sen's representation of them which forms the crux of this book.

From a study of the four most representative women-centric Hindi films from the 1940s to the '70s: *Andaz* (1949), *Dhool ka Phool* (1959), *Mother India* (1957) and

Aradhana (1969), one can discern the position of women in society as well as how the world viewed them.

In *Andaz*, for instance, Neena is a young woman whose modern upbringing makes her open and vivacious, but also temperamental. One day, her runaway horse gets rescued by a young man called Dilip who promptly falls in love with her. She becomes friendly with him; one may even think that she is encouraging him. However, it is soon revealed that there is a young man in her life; he arrives in India after completing his studies abroad and the two get married.

In the course of the narrative, Dilip confesses to his love for Neena and this makes her life go awry. She begins to feel pangs of guilt, and her married life begins to suffer as she finds herself unable to be happy anymore. To make matters worse, her husband begins to suspect her and takes his daughter away to live with him, having cast aspersions on her character. Very soon, a crisis ensues when Dilip, crazed with love and passion for Neena, tries to physically assault her. She kills him in self-defence and faces a sentence for life in the process, after her husband denounces her as a murderer.

What is interesting is the way the woman has been represented in this film. In the films examined here, motherhood becomes a key focus, as do marriage and living the life of an ideal wife and woman. This is expressed through sartorial changes in the woman's representation, along with behavioural changes. While the husband's outward behaviour remains the same before and after marriage, he is shown as an indulgent father. Society, through the figure of Neena's husband and other men, expects her to behave in a particular way. Failing to adhere to these norms brings ruin to her life. The film serves as a didactic lesson for all Indian women—illustrating the consequences Neena faces when she fails to follow societal expectations.

In *Dhool ka Phool* (1959), the question of motherhood rears its head once again. Only this time, it is an unmarried mother who, unable to bear the brunt of shame, decides to give away her child. Her only living relatives—her aunt and uncle—turn her out of the house, and her nursemaid gives her shelter. Soon, she too leaves this world while Meena is left alone with the child. When she abandons the child in a forest, a kind Muslim man passing by adopts him and brings him up as his own.

In the meantime, Meena's lover and the biological father of her child is forced to get married to a rich man's daughter. He settles down and forges a successful career as a magistrate. Interestingly, the man in such narratives is never blamed for the outrage caused to the woman. However, in this film, despite being blessed with a good and devoted wife, he loses his only son to an accident in a moment of poetic justice of sorts.

Meena, on the other hand, is blessed with a successful advocate for a husband, who also forgives her 'transgression' and readily accepts her son as his own. This film, much like *Aradhana* which I discuss next, is one of those that portray women with a modern outlook, who are not afraid to be intimate with their suitors before marriage (considered sacred by Indian society). However, at the same time, these films deem it necessary to punish these women. The women in such narratives are usually shown as victims, rather than strong, empowered women. Their 'deliverance' almost always lies with a man, usually another kindred soul, or their sons. While these films are generally reflective of what Indian society is like, nevertheless, the director's treatment of the woman protagonist always follows a particular script.

In *Aradhana* (1969) by Shakti Samanta, the story is once again of an unwed mother played by Sharmila Tagore. Once again, the woman is shown to 'transgress' with respect to Indian values when there is a promise of marriage.

Vandana, a beautiful young woman, is accosted by a handsome young pilot played by Rajesh Khanna, the leading superstar of the day, and the two fall in love after a brief courtship. The man, being honourable and having indulged in physical intimacies with the woman, decides to marry her and take her home so that they can start a family together. They do get married in a temple with God as witness as is the wont in Hindi film narratives, but before a social marriage can take place, the man dies. She is refused access to his house or property by his scheming aunt, and the uncle who has no voice simply disappears.

She gives birth to her son Suraj, and when a wealthy couple adopts him, she chooses to stay close to him by working as his nanny. Everything seems fine until Shyam, a relative, begins to harass her, eventually attempting to assault her. In her defence, Suraj stabs him, but she takes the blame and ends up in jail.

Here again, the woman is depicted more as a victim. Her overarching ambition in life is to see her son become a pilot, thus realizing his father's ambition for him. She is ready to comply with this dream to the extent of even going to jail for the sake of her son. She is also represented as chaste, and sincere to the memory of her dead fiancé. The dominant image one carries away from the viewing of *Aradhana* is that of a long-suffering woman, forever pitted against the Fates. Her deliverance is only granted when Suraj, her son, grows up to become a pilot and recognizes her sacrifice.

Mother India (1957), a film celebrated for several reasons, once again has a woman at the centre of the plot. Radha, the protagonist, marries into her husband's family with his mother having borrowed money from the local moneylender, Sukhilala. This is where begins their tale of woe. Since the whole family is uneducated, they are unable to make sense of the conniving Lala's schemes and calculations, and go on repaying his loan by handing over to him 20 bighas of their land at first, followed by one-third of their crop share.

Radha's husband loses his hands in a freak accident when a boulder lands on them and crush them as they are trying to make a piece of land ploughable. He feels ashamed about the fact that he can no longer feed his family, and not wanting to be a burden on them, disappears from their lives. Radha is left alone to bring up her two young sons. While Ramu, the older one, is calm and goes to school to study, Birju, the younger one, shows signs of rebellion from a very young age.

There are several images of Radha putting in a great deal of hard work and physical labour to help her husband. Needless to say, these shots are always framed in a particular way—highlighting Radha's sacrifice and always portraying her sweating face against a searing sun, thus emphasising her pain and valour.

When the film opens, she is an old woman whose life has not just been full of pain and suffering from physical hardships, but she has also killed her younger son Birju because he violated the honour of a village belle. Radha called the woman the honour of the village and challenged her son to disobey her. Full of anger, he did it because he had always been a hot-headed person and acted without giving too much thought to anything.

Birju's trajectory is marked by his inability to reconcile his grievances with the village's values. His antics escalate into violence, culminating in his transformation into a bandit. The climactic sequence where Birju returns on the day of Sukhilala's daughter's wedding to exact vengeance epitomizes his inner turmoil. His killing of Sukhilala liberates the village from the latter's tyranny, but his abduction of the moneylender's daughter crosses the line of honour. True to her principles, Radha fulfils her promise to protect the village's dignity by shooting her son, and holding his lifeless body as the ultimate testament to her unwavering resolve. The woman, without fail, is deemed an exemplar, an icon of the village, for having kept her word. Even though she works extremely hard for her sons' upbringing, she doesn't fail to punish Birju when the time comes. Just as the film's title suggests, she stands for the nation in the post-Independence period, trying to stand on her own two feet, while the film can be read as an allegory of the young nation trying to find its place in the world. Although she is a mother, the film seems to say that as a person who is looked up to and respected by others, she must make the ultimate sacrifice if called upon to do so.

Art Cinema

While the concept of the 'ideal feminine' existed and was propagated in Indian cinema, parallel cinema followed quite a different trajectory. Rather than disseminating a unified picture of a utopian Indian culture, it sought to generate insight into Indian life by capturing the experiences and contradictions of a society in transition, by focusing on small segments of Indian reality, exploring complex layers of meaning at the same time. A new type of woman emerged from this kind of cinema, one who was very different from the traditional heroines of commercial cinema. She was placed in several different contexts, confronting a multiplicity of social problems besieging Indian society.

The parallel cinema movement was funded by the Film Finance Corporation (FFC), a government organ, which naturally meant that their agendas would often be pre-decided. The plots of these films revolved around ordinary people, as opposed to the often mindless escapism of popular cinema.

The first two films which heralded the beginning of this movement were Basu Chatterjee's *Sara Aakash* and Mrinal Sen's *Bhuvan Shome*, both released in 1969. Both these films were considered as role models for the later middle cinema which would follow. While both Chatterjee and Aparna Sen's emphasis was on simplicity and authenticity, a subtle change was noted in the films of Hrishikesh Mukherjee, Gulzar, Basu Bhattacharya as well as the later Basu Chatterjee in that they attempted to be entertaining as well.

Shyam Benegal's *Bhumika* was a film in which Usha was a nominally strong woman character. In fact, Benegal made several films with women protagonists—*Mammo* (1994), *Sardari Begum* (1996), *Zubeidaa* (2001), to name a few. However, the issue of agency being a requisite part of women's emancipation was never much of a concern in any of these films.

If one were to study these closely, they would see that the fight was against an all-pervasive system (unnamed but symbolized by one or several characters). One could even say that too many issues were being investigated, such as those of poverty, social injustice, the brutal subjugation of the lower castes and women, and the orthodoxies of tradition.

Usha, the protagonist of *Bhumika,* is a successful film actress, but she has a bad family life, namely a husband who is suspicious, orthodox and unemployed. She is the sole breadwinner of the family, but is not able to exercise much choice in any matter. One day, having had enough, she decides to walk out of her marital home, but then drifts from one relationship to another. It is also not clear why she chooses to marry her husband Keshav Dehalvi in the first place when they clearly do not share any kind of compatibility.

The director chooses to highlight Usha's various relationships to point out how each of them fails her and her expectations of them. In between, there are several shots of her working life which fulfils her in a way that family life cannot. Released in 1977, the film must have come across as a powerful feminist statement to various members of the audience. However, a close scrutiny of the film never yields much about Usha's inner life, apart from external manifestations thereof in the form of disagreements with her husband and many of her lovers.

Unlike Aparna Sen's protagonist Mrinalini in her film *Iti Mrinalini*, Usha does not reveal her vulnerable side. As a working woman in a male-dominated industry, Usha is bound to have faced discrimination simply because of her sex, but Benegal never makes us privy to anything uncomfortable. Much of the blame is laid on the men populating the narrative, and that is how Benegal wishes to express his support for the woman. The real questions never get to be asked.

When Usha lands up in a remote manor house as a chatelaine and feels imprisoned because of her lover's imperious ways, she has to take recourse to calling her husband to rescue her. Her lover's wife accepts her because she realizes that as a person with disability, she cannot fulfil her husband's sexual desires; hence her acceptance of her husband's paramour. It highlights the conditions of women in a feudal society. *Iti Mrinalini*, which resembles Benegal's story of a woman who decides to take matters into her own hands when her marital relationship fails, has a far more courageous heroine—one who is perhaps on her way to emancipation as we envisage it. When her relationship with her lover Siddhartha Sarkar fails, Mrinalini decides to move on while the man is left feeling grievously injured because of that.

In case of most of Usha's relationships in *Bhumika*, the men in her life either leave her or make life so unbearable for her that within a short span of time she is forced to leave them. None of the relationships portrayed seem to have any depth, and last for only short periods of time. The only right decision the excitable Usha takes while exhibiting some kind of agency is that of living life alone at the end of the narrative. She chooses neither to be with her husband who seems to have turned over a new leaf, nor with her daughter, now a grown-up young woman with a family of her own.

Umbartha (1982) by Jabbar Patel, once again, portrays a strong female lead played by Smita Patil. However, the trajectory of Sulabha Mahajan's life is very different from that of Usha's. She is an advocate's wife who is bored of her life as a housewife and decides to take up a job in another town. At first, the husband is quite supportive, while her older sister-in-law pitches in to help look after her young daughter. Having a master's degree in social work, Sulabha decides to try her hand at a job at a women's correctional home. She is extremely successful at her job. Confronted by challenges posed by corruption and the exploitation of the women, which plays a major role in ruining women's lives, she rises to the occasion magnificently. Having been shunned by society and their families, these women expect to be protected by the high walls of the correctional home and the state; however, even the state plays a major role in perpetuating the exploitation of these destitute women. From here onwards, Sulabha's personal and inner life ceases to be a point of interest and her life at the correctional home assumes primary importance, although it was quite clear at the beginning that this was going to be her story.

Jabbar Patel's camera begins to zoom in on the lives of the inmates with Sulabha's professional life coming into sharper focus. No longer is she the bored wife from a comparatively rich family, leading an easy life. She gets up early in the mornings and works hard until the late hours of the night. She seems to have been granted a fresh lease of life which she wants to make full use of. Her familial and personal life seems to hold no special meaning for her while she is at work. As a result of this, her young daughter refuses to recognize her at the end of the narrative, while her husband seems to have established physical relations with another woman, which he expects his wife to understand and accept.

Was the director then trying to say that this was a price that professional and dedicated women must pay if they devoted more time to work? Or was he simply lamenting the fact that such a thing befell the conscientious and hardworking Sulabha? Either way, Patel's film broke new ground because one fails to come up with the name of any such film in commercial cinema in which the woman's professional life was highlighted to such a degree.

Ritwik Ghatak, Rituparno Ghosh and Aparna Sen: Art Cinema in Bengal

Ritwik Ghatak was associated with the Indian People's Theatre Association (IPTA) before he decided to become a full-fledged filmmaker. This association connected him with Aparna Sen as well. Several of his films contained women protagonists around whose lives the narratives revolved. His films remain a few of the most powerful artistic articulations of the trauma of displacement in the wake of the Partition. As an artist, he found it difficult to accept the Partition and it became an obsession with him, featuring as a recurring theme in his work. In his lifetime, he made only eight feature films as opposed to his more prolific contemporaries.

Most of his films depicted the plight of people affected by the Partition through heightened melodrama, while his contemporary Satyajit Ray—whose oeuvre displayed great versatility in terms of subject as well as treatment—was subtle. His other contemporary Mrinal Sen, on the other hand, was more direct in his approach.

Meghe Dhaka Tara (1960), one of Ghatak's most acclaimed films, deals with the story of Neeta, the sole breadwinner in a family of refugees. She sacrifices everything for her family while they exploit her good nature and take advantage of her. Her father who tries to protest on her behalf is often ignored, while her elder brother who loves her deeply is unable to support her because he is unemployed, and therefore has no say in anything. She is dealt a heavy blow by her lover who betrays her by choosing to marry her younger sister instead. She is devastated and develops tuberculosis, and must be put in a sanatorium. The film has an open ending but what is significant is the way Ghatak portrays his protagonist—therein lies his sympathy as a director. In his other films, *Komal Gandhar* (1961) and *Subarnarekha* (1962), although the focus is on the Partition of Bengal (an overarching theme in his films), there are important women characters who drive the narrative forward.

Unlike commercial Hindi or Bengali cinema, the women here are not merely objects of desire and love; instead, they are women in their own rights within the frame of the narrative. They often drive the narrative forward, as in the case of *Meghe Dhaka Tara*. The subjugation of women and casteist practices of the Bengali *bhadralok* community were also explored by Ghatak in his films. This preoccupation with the Bengali bhadralok was also taken up by Rituparno Ghosh later, and he explored various facets thereof in his films. Again, several of his films contained strong female leads and there was an overwhelming urge to understand the world of women.

Ghosh went on to become one of Bengal's most successful film directors after the passing of Ray. He followed in the footsteps of Ray, who he claimed was a huge influence on him. To a certain extent, Ghosh himself became a cult figure because of his films. Ghosh's portrayal of women consists of emancipated working women who undergo emotional turmoil of various sorts. For instance, one of his earliest films *Unishe April* deals with the relationship of a mother-daughter duo. Sarojini, the mother, is a successful danseuse, and her daughter Aditi is a doctor who has a somewhat difficult relationship with the former. Egged on by a dissatisfied husband and channelized as a weapon, the young girl grows up hating her mother. However, at the moment the film opens, Aditi is in a turbulent relationship with her lover who refuses to marry her because her mother is a dancer, which is not seen as a respectable profession by conservative middle-class Bengalis.

Dahan (1997), for instance, is an adaptation of Suchitra Bhattacharya's novel of the same name, which was based on an actual incident of molestation of a young woman in Kolkata. The film is a sensitive portrayal of the same onscreen. Whereas the audience for the book was limited, the narrative went on to receive a far wider audience when adapted to the silver screen. Time and again, Ghosh tried to address the complexities of relationships, emotional intricacies as well as the silent struggles that are inherent in everyday life.

Ghosh's cinematic tradition consists of a deep study of patriarchy, the feminine identity, and the complexities of human emotion, and followed in the creative footsteps of Satyajit Ray. The majority of Ghosh's films revolve around the politics of the home and the struggle of individuals within the domestic space to negotiate with the conventions of the traditional joint family and work through the everyday intricacies of marital and/or mother-child relationships, as in *Unishe April* and *Titli* (2002).

Gendered agency and subjectivity are complex questions which Rituparno Ghosh, alongside other (mostly art-house) film directors, tried to address. Along with Ghosh, Aparna Sen, to a certain extent, also grappled with these subjects as a detailed examination of her films will show. In Bengal, Ghosh and Sen are synonymous with the progressive cinema made in the vein of the trio—Satyajit Ray, Ritwik Ghatak and Mrinal Sen.

Of course, being a woman, both Sen's subject matter and treatment are more nuanced when it comes to dealing with women subjects. The strength of Sen's films lies in the very fact that the women find a way to live even within the dominant discourse, and often from outside it. In her cinema, women come to symbolize traditional values as well as the strategic undermining thereof. Sen's strength lies in the fact that she does not deny modernity as her characters confront traditional values and struggle to negotiate the 'visibility' and 'invisibility' quotients in their existence, positions and roles in society. These women constantly reinterpret restrictive, traditional ideologies, thus helping to put forth the idea that traditional expectations from women in a modern society are unrealistic.

Invoking Love, Death and an Elsewhere

36 Chowringhee Lane

Aparna Sen's debut film is about an Anglo-Indian spinster called Miss Violet Stoneham who decides to remain in post-Independence India while her other relatives and friends leave for Canada, Australia or Britain. The film revolves around her life, and especially her relationship with a former student Nandita and her boyfriend Samaresh. The narrative of the film spans a year and Sen depicts her as a terribly lonely figure through the initial section of the film.

The chirping of birds, the honking car horns, the footsteps on the busy streets of Calcutta, juxtaposed with the stillness of the cemetery, the ringing of the morning bells in the school, the siren from a factory, the humdrum sounds of life being lived is how *36 Chowringhee Lane* opens. The protagonist is an aged woman—almost a first for Indian cinema. Her daily life revolves around a handful of activities: teaching William Shakespeare's *Twelfth Night*, taking care of her cat Sir Toby, writing letters to her niece, and visiting the cemetery to pay respects to her loved ones.

Every Thursday, she brings chocolate biscuits and Archie comics to her brother Eddie, who is unwell and stays in an old-age home. From time to time, she allows herself a small treat by visiting the fish market to buy prawns—a modest luxury and her one indulgence.

When Nandita and Samaresh come into her life, she makes conscious efforts to fit in and belong. As film scholar M.K. Raghavendra states,[9] Aparna Sen's debut film is perhaps one of the best examples of an English film in India, and therefore, it comes as no surprise that it would tell the story of the community that speaks this very language—the Anglo-Indians. Apart from Satyajit Ray's sensitive portrayal of the Anglo-Indians through the character of Edith in *Mahanagar*,[10] very few films dealt with them, and yet at one point of time, they were a prominent community in Calcutta. They were like the living vestiges of the British Raj who quite reverently held on to high culture. Therefore, it comes as no surprise that Miss Stoneham is an English teacher teaching Shakespeare in a girls' school.

The Alienated Self

Miss Violet Stoneham's identity as neither an Indian citizen nor a British one makes her feel alienated, as does her financial status—clearly reflected in the state of her abode

[9]Raghavendra, M.K., *50 Indian Film Classics*, HarperCollins, India, 2009, p. 223.

[10]A sympathetic, rather an empathetic, portrayal of an Anglo-Indian woman by Satyajit Ray in his 1962 film *Mahanagar,* which is nothing short of brilliant. Subtle as always, he portrayed the xenophobic attitude of Bengalis, here exemplified by Arati and Edith's boss Mr Mukherjee.

and the wistful and longing looks she casts at the prawns on display at the fish market. She lives a simple life that is monotonous and perhaps even dull. To establish her tedious and dreary existence, the shots of her flat are portrayed in dark overtones with hardly any light filtering in. While the shots of her at work do include light streaming in from large windows, they are juxtaposed with shots of students who couldn't be bothered with her teaching. While she teaches *Twelfth Night*, the students are mostly seen chatting, passing notes to one another or reading comics.

Miss Stoneham has a cat for a companion, whom she calls Sir Toby, a character from *Twelfth Night*, who does not seem to demand food or affection. A saucer of milk suffices for him while he and Miss Stoneham continue spending their evenings together companionably. The house she lives in is dank and gloomy. It is an old apartment block with a lift that is perpetually out of order, which is also an oblique comment on Miss Stoneham's own situation. Her home consists of two small rooms and a tiny kitchen with which she seems satisfied, but throughout the narrative, her mind keeps harking back to old memories, triggered sometimes by letters from her niece in Australia, another time by the presence of Nandita and Samaresh in her house.

The only recurring theme in her life is the absence of her lover and fiancé Davy who died in the war. The memories, and to be more precise, her repressed sexuality, are triggered when she sees Nandita and Samaresh in an intimate embrace. The dream sequences in *36 Chowringhee Lane* are stark and invoke pathos—a young Violet is looking for her lover Davy in a forest when she comes across a door on the other side of which a dream and a nightmare unfold simultaneously. A funeral and a wedding ceremony overlap with each other. The wedding vows and the prayer for the dead are all mixed up—a happy occasion is juxtaposed with a truly terrifying one. Life and death merge and collapse in this sequence. This assumes a special significance—Violet Stoneham is trapped in a limbo: alive yet buried.

In fact, the film begins with shots of gravestones, wildflowers and the protagonist visiting the graves accompanied by bouquets. As she lingers near one, the camera zooms in on it, revealing the name 'Davy'. Her weekly visits to her older brother Eddie at an old-age home do not cheer her up. In fact, she seems to be scared by the prospect of old age and haunted by the visages of the elderly at the home.

It is on a Christmas morning that she meets the strolling lovers, her former student Nandita and her boyfriend Samaresh, in the Maidan as she is walking back from Mass, and this meeting does much to quell her loneliness. For the first time, her life does not seem to be predictable and dry, but filled with laughter and happiness. Her pursed lips, the constant frown on her forehead, her pensive eyes and trembling hands disappear when she is with her new friends. For her, their presence is like a breath of fresh air. She no longer has to return to just an empty home and a cat.

While her niece Rosemary keeps writing to her with news of herself and her family, she keeps imploring Miss Stoneham to come and live with them in Australia. However, the latter resolutely refuses to listen to sound advice because of her brother Eddie, or so she tells herself. As she pores over Rosemary's letters, her thoughts once again go back to the past (flashbacks being the mode via which we learn of Miss Stoneham's past) when Rosemary was younger and very much in love with an upper-caste Bengali boy who wanted to marry her. When his cultured family resisted, she was forced to marry an Anglo-Indian boy Cedric out of fear that her life would also be reduced to one of pain, longing and unfulfilled desires—like her aunt's. She married and quickly migrated to Australia when her husband moved abroad for work.

Back to the present, the young upper-class Bengali couple are bored (with Samaresh running out of money) of necking in taxis while looking for a room in which to get intimate. Even as Miss Stoneham lends them her very private space—a private world, ostensibly for Samaresh to write in—in return she gets to enjoy their company and is welcomed home every day with a cup of hot tea which Nandita prepares for her. While the couple enjoy sex under the pretext of Samaresh writing his debut novel and creating a magnum opus, the months which whizz by are idyllic for Miss Stoneham, who does not suspect anything. No longer confined to lonely evenings or a weekly visit to her cranky brother Eddie who demands Miss Stoneham's attention and affection in the form of chocolate biscuits despite being unwell, Miss Stoneham now spends her time with Nandita and her boyfriend, laughing and enjoying ice cream and *phuchkas*.

Desperate for human contact, Miss Stoneham ignores their repeated slights until she walks in on a naked Samaresh and Nandita, which demystifies any sense of romanticism she had built around their friendship. The film lingers around these idyllic, fun memories, capturing every small moment—alternating between a comparatively happy Miss Stoneham at work, who even begins to smile, a complete contrast to earlier images of her as a glum and sad person, and the deliriously happy couple who can, for the first time, have sex any time of the day which now moves faster.

Just like her staid lectures on the extremely enjoyable and lively play *Twelfth Night*, she seems satisfied to be living the life of a voyeur. Instead of being an active participant in life, she seems content in living the one she has in the old apartment, while Samaresh and Nandita fleece her with their little gifts and sweet talk. The highlight of the film (if one could call it that) is perhaps the way the young couple go about fooling the old lady, cashing in on her loneliness, her need to be loved, and perhaps her predilection for English literature. While Samaresh, in his first meeting with Miss Stoneham, is extremely put off because he cannot indulge in physical intimacies with Nandita, he comes around very soon when he manages to impress Miss Stoneham into giving them access to the flat. He wilfully lies to her by calling himself a poet and a novelist of the order of James Joyce, and fooled by terms such as patronage, patrons and the like, Miss Stoneham begins to dream of herself as one and decides to lend her flat to the budding novelist.

Miss Stoneham is treated most shabbily by Nandita and Samaresh who do not find any use for her when they are married. They are now preoccupied in their own world; Samaresh has a well-paying job and they have moved to a big house which Nandita's parents gifted the couple. They no longer have any need for Miss Stoneham's company, nor her flat, and do not have time to humour her anymore. Violet Stoneham, therefore, must return to her solitude, her own company and that of Sir Toby's. She is also divested of her gramophone when she gifts it to them as a wedding present, and along with it, the last remnant of music in her life. Her unconditional love and friendship (not to speak of being a good and kind hostess to them) was already reduced to a relationship of patronage, as Samaresh called it, and it was no longer required. As she leaves them behind, she recites from Shakespeare's *King Lear* a passage that evokes his blindness—his inability to see people for what they truly are. Did Miss Stoneham make a similar mistake? Did she trust the wrong people after all?

The Bengali couple's rejection of Miss Stoneham rings as true as Mr Mukherjee's rejection of Edith in Satyajit Ray's *Mahanagar*, where he displays a racist and misogynistic aversion towards her. However, Arati, the protagonist who considers Edith a friend, shows unusual courage and displays female camaraderie by resigning from her job when Edith is fired. In Miss Violet Stoneham's case, nobody is around to show her any support except a cur at Victoria Memorial when she likens her life to that of Lear. While the film ends on a note of dejection, one is not sure whether Miss Stoneham will now move to Australia to be with Rosemary. Even as she unhappily listens to talks about her other colleagues' lives in the West or their plans to move to pastures new, she makes no move to follow suit.

The Betrayal and the Failure of Relationships

The time frame for the film is a year—from one Christmas Eve to the next Christmas when it closes. As the camera roves over the city, one becomes aware of the city as a living entity as well—almost an antagonist to Miss Stoneham which is determined to force her out. The camera wanders over both the rich and the homeless while 'Silent Night' plays over the soundtrack, setting off an ironic contradiction. And in the midst of this charged public sphere is Sen's protagonist Miss Stoneham who is the lonely outsider. While Christmas is her festival, ironically it is the richer Indians who celebrate it with cake and pastries from Flury's and parties at home. She, on the other hand, must make do with a small cake from a local shop, with Nandita and Samaresh for company.

The next Christmas, when Miss Stoneham visits the couple after they are married, they are unsurprisingly rude to her. They appear cold and indifferent and are eager to get rid of her by pretending to be busy. Miss Stoneham, who still believes in the tenets of friendship, decides to bring them a homemade fruitcake for Christmas despite their protests that they wouldn't be in Calcutta. She persists, and in the end, is greeted by a Christmas party being held by the couple from which she has been excluded. Cake still in her tote, she makes a martyred exit.

In portraying Miss Stoneham the way she did, Aparna Sen seemed to be making a political statement of sorts. Her alienation would be complete by the end of the narrative when Nandita and Samaresh reject her.

Aparna Sen foregrounds her protagonist's private life to externalize the public tension—that between independent

Indians and the community which reminded them of their colonial past. Miss Stoneham and the likes of her at large felt displaced and left behind, as if they were the living 'ghosts' of a forgettable past. As Indians tried to make the most of the opportunities available to them in an independent India, they began to replace Miss Stoneham's very community, where once they were the teachers, the translators and the compilers of useful works. Miss Stoneham begins to feel rejected when she is demoted to teaching English grammar to junior schoolgirls, while the Shakespeare classes are taken up by a younger, more educated Bengali woman who joins the staff.

It also highlights their hypocrisy in having no qualms in using the colonizer's language for their own gain, or in utilizing the benefits that an English education gives them. The couple's betrayal of Miss Stoneham is also symbolically highlighted by the scene in which her long-cherished antique gramophone, now Nandita and Samaresh's wedding present, plays 'Lipstick on your Collar' and 'A House of Bamboo' to revellers at their Christmas party, of which she becomes a mere voyeur instead of a cherished guest.

However, instead of treating Miss Stoneham as a lone Christian martyr, the forsaken woman, Sen suggests that her audience read her as a dignified, last remaining vestige of British India, and not a victim. Sen's obsessive focus on the tiniest of details in Miss Stoneham's life never turns didactic. Instead, it becomes a careful documentation of the life of a person whose community is slowly fading out from public life. Even as she enters the last frame, we hear her composing a letter to Rosemary contemplating leaving the land of her birth, and even as her defeat seems imminent, we are made privy to her rendering of the lines from *King Lear*, fashioning her into a stoic figure who is not yet ready to accept defeat.

Sen's film is a subtle representation of an individual living on the fringes of mainstream post-Independence Indian society. Even while the audience feels her rejection at the hands of her Indian friends as unfair, the film does not implicate Samaresh and Nandita in any way. Instead, Sen seems to be saying that people are what they are and they do what they do because of that. However, it leaves one with the sense that Sen's film bears the imprint of a feminine aesthetic of resistance, and one which will come to have a bearing on the rest of her oeuvre as well.

Iti Mrinalini

How does one think or even begin to write about a film that has autobiographical elements from the director's life? While this certainly would not be the first time that Sen included elements from her life in her films, this one seems to have an explicit resemblance to her own life as an actress, and more importantly, a commercial film actress. Aparna Sen's 2010 directorial venture is about an actress past her prime, who decides to take her own life after being disappointed in love yet again. She feels rejected as a woman and an actress. In the last third of the film, the actress spends the whole night remembering past events of her life and, as the first light of the morning appears, and along with it, a text on her phone from her best friend Chintan, she decides that suicide is not the answer.

The film takes recourse to a series of flashbacks to reveal Mrinalini's life to the viewer, and we see her evolution from a simple middle-class college girl with actorly ambitions to a mature and sophisticated woman and successful commercial film actress. While we have her story in the foreground, we also have bits of the history of the city as well as that of Bengali cinema in the background (commercial versus art cinema, references to Satyajit Ray, Ritwik Ghatak and Mrinal Sen, and so on). The film is unusual in that no film director would readily take on the subject of an ageing actress's life. In this, the film bears resemblance to Shyam Benegal's *Bhumika*, yet it differs from it on many counts. Sen unflinchingly holds up a mirror to some of the actress's most vulnerable moments in her film career.

Sen's story is set in the world of cinema, but the film is not so much about her life as an actress as it is about her relationships with men. The milieu only provides her with the opportunity to meet and bond with unusual people. On the one hand, Mrinalini has money and fame, but on the other hand, she has neither a family nor a steady loving presence in her life. But we admire her for being an individual and making her own choices. Although she passes through a series of difficulties, a ray of hope in the story comes from Chintan Nair, who tells her that there are different kinds of love, and she should not expect that she would be loved exactly the way she wants to be loved.

The film begins with a mature Mrinalini who has just received critical acclaim for her portrayal of Kunti. Sen's film moves back and forth in time as she sits contemplating death while tearing up old letters and photographs of her daughter Sohini with her lover, who had refused to marry her. As she takes up each object in her hand, they bring back vivid memories while revealing her past to us little by little. These stories are told in a chronological manner.

She picks up a book of poems titled *Smritir Shohor* by Sunil Gangopadhyay, gifted to her by her young classmate and lover Abhi. There is a flashback to a lively scene in which a young Mrinalini sits surrounded by her friends in a coffee house, typical of the Bengali youth and intellectuals. The time is the late 1960s when Naxalism was at its height in Calcutta. Abhi is a known offender to the police, but that does not deter him from loudly professing his political ideology. Mrinalini is content to lead the life of a college-goer in front of her other friends, but to Abhi, she reveals the tensions at home, the inevitability of her being married off and a future of financial dependence. She announces to him her determination to be a Bengali commercial film heroine. Eager to escape the tensions at home and fuelled by a determination to find a 'room' of her own, she decides to give up her studies and fend for herself.

Sen's protagonist comes across as someone determined to succeed on her own terms. However, to do that, she has to sacrifice her lofty ideals of acting in a Satyajit Ray film or those reminiscent of the works of her favourite film directors—François Truffaut, Jean-Luc Godard, Federico Fellini, and so on. She comes across as diffident, shy and a little too naïve when Sumitra Devi, a slightly older and successful contemporary actress, jealous of Mrinalini's acting prowess, gets rid of her from her next film *Durgeshnandini* in which both of them were to act together, and in which Mrinalini was sure to have excelled.

It is extremely interesting to note that Sen tries to uphold the Bengali tendency of filming adaptations and the very literary quality of the region's cinema. Most of the films in which Mrinalini acts in her early days are adapted from Bankim Chandra Chatterjee's novels. Some of the shots from Mrinalini's films, as portrayed by Sen, are reminiscent of her own films as a commercial film heroine. These exemplify the personal elements in the film and Sen's particular style of filmmaking.

Of Friendship and Failed Relationships

Right from the beginning of her life, Mrinalini felt abandoned by her father who left his family, consisting of his wife and two young children—something which seems to have traumatized her mother no end. Perhaps it is a protective father figure that she searches for her entire life but, just like her father, the men in her life seem to fail her in one way or another.

Abhi also 'abandons' her—when he dies at the hands of the Calcutta Police in an 'encounter'. It is perhaps his untimely death that haunts her the most in an unconscious way, her whole life—for it is one of the principal things which she recalls as she prepares herself for death. And it is also precisely in the same manner that she meets her own end—shot (accidentally) from behind by a bullet intended for another as she is walking her dog early one morning.

The one relationship in her life in which she feels comforted and assured of is the one between her and Chintan. At various stages of her life, when she feels betrayed, it is to Chintan that she turns. He is perhaps the only man in her life who does not get into a conventional romantic relationship with her, and yet, is someone who loves her dearly. Perhaps it is this very thing which keeps the relationship going—even at the last moment when she is about to give up her life, abandoned by all.

Eventually, another man—Siddhartha Sarkar—comes into Mrinalini's life and is drawn into her inner world as someone who understands her completely and someone with whom she can share her innermost thoughts.

Siddhartha Sarkar seems to be the quintessential creative artist who does not hesitate to take advantage of a naïve protégée when available; so Mrinalini becomes his mistress of sorts while he finds it difficult to leave his family and start afresh with her. Through this, Sen seems to be suggesting that Siddhartha—shackled as he is in patriarchal mores—finds it difficult to do anything unconventional that would invite criticism from many quarters while a woman has the courage to go the extra mile, and that perhaps such courage can only be found in women.

Even though Sen does not provide the backstory for Mrinalini's involvement with a married man, one can surmise that it was perhaps because she had a close working relationship with him. The absence of a guardian figure also robs her of good guidance, which is necessary in a world of cut-throat competition, such as cinema. However, in professional matters, she seems to make all the correct choices.

Much in the vein of sundry cinematic narratives, Siddhartha and she marry each other in a temple, which is considered illegitimate in the eyes of the law. Citing various excuses at different times, Siddhartha wriggles out of uncomfortable situations with Mrinalini who insists that he marry her. He doesn't, and she remains the eternal outsider.

Before Mrinalini finally decides to call it off, they have a child together. However, she feels angry and frustrated at his dishonesty and refusal to commit. She also decides to bring up their child Sohini as a single mother when her daughter expresses a desire to live with her. The child shows an unprecedented degree of maturity, intelligence and sensitivity when she calmly states the fact to Mrinalini that she knows that Siddhartha and Mrinalini are her parents.

Over time, the mother and daughter develop a tender bond—even though they do not share a usual mother-daughter relationship, as Mrinalini cannot claim her as a biological daughter for fear of a backlash from the media. Sen's film seems to indicate that a woman's desire for love and companionship is a sacrifice that she must make for success while gaining an identity of her own. Mrinalini Mitra attains success and becomes a household name with her debut film, and goes on to have an extremely successful career. But her success also makes her headstrong and determined to live life on her own terms.

Years later, when Imtiaz Choudhary, a US-returned film director, approaches her for a role, reluctant at first, she gives in because of her craving for good roles as an artist. Is it because she still hopes to find the happiness which has eluded her all her life? The nature of their relationship is not very clear, but the two seem to bond over the course of the film *Born of the Sun*—a modern take on Tagore's poem 'Karna Kunti Sambad'. Perhaps she comes to depend on Imtiaz and even begins to trust him enough to think of a new beginning with him, both as an actress and a woman. However, even before they can begin, she gets an indication of Imtiaz's interest in the younger heroine—Hiya Mazumdar—who plays the role of Draupadi, and with whom he is contemplating making another film. When the producers announce this new venture with Hiya as the heroine, she feels betrayed, but more so by the revelation that he was never personally interested in her. She spends most of her time alone at the film's premier party when she begins to feel a sense of being abandoned once again. No one seems particularly bothered about her exit from the party and she decides to take her life that very same night. Her untimely death would perhaps help grab some headlines for her—something that has eluded her for a long time.

In 2010, Rituparno Ghosh made a film called *Abohomaan* on a director's relationship with his actress. But the film recounted the perspectives of the son and the wife of the director, and the whole narrative focused on the tension unfolding in the director's family because of the affair, but the relationship between the director and the younger heroine was not delineated in detail. The crises within the family—the husband and wife's estrangement and the son distancing himself from the father—formed the crux of Rituparno's narrative. As Rituparno said of his film, 'My main interest was to unfold for myself, as much as for my actors and my audience, the finer nuances of the relationship between the creator and the created, what are the elements that sustain it, and why such relationships finally do not hold in time.'[11] A complex web of relationships overlap; the conflict between the various members of the director's family is apparently resolved with his death.

The various relationships in the film take up screen time without focusing on Sikha, Aniket's heroine, or her evolution from a brash, little educated, unsophisticated theatre actress living in north Calcutta (which Aniket's wife

---

[11]Interview with Kaustav Bakshi.

Deepti pointedly calls our attention to) to a successful film actress. Only towards the end of the film does Aniket's son seek out Sikha to find out more about her and his father's relationship. Clearly, the focus is on this singular aspect of the director's life, unlike Aparna Sen's film whose entire focus is on Mrinalini's life.

The only other Indian director who has attempted filming such a subject is Shyam Benegal. In a society where women are not viewed as important members, the fact that Sen wished to examine a woman's life is laudatory. Aparna's gaze is on Mrinalini; it is her perspective through which we look at the world and the people in it. It is literally her voice which permeates the narrative. Her suicide note is the first document which greets the audience, and which also sets the tenor of the film: to expect the unexpected.

In *Iti Mrinalini* too, just as in *36 Chowringhee Lane,* Mrinalini's interior world is explored—first through her disappointing love life and family life, and then her professional life. There is a great deal of focus on her relationship with Siddhartha Sarkar even as Sen's camera weaves in and out between the private and the public, and by public, I mean the face she presents to the world at large. Interestingly, the sociopolitical background of the events is never explored. We just get a faint whiff of the Naxal movement at work when we see her lover Abhi killed in a police encounter on the Maidan, and from the walls covered with political graffiti and slogans while she is still a student.

Once her professional life begins, one has no indication of the political reality of the decades during which she is working, as the narrative begins to concentrate a great deal on her personal life. In *Iti Mrinalini*, physical spaces are not of as much importance as states of the mind. 'Mrinalini' being a part of the title of the film seems to suggest that she is the world around which the plot revolves. It is through her eyes that we see the world as well as view the world. Although treated sympathetically, the character is not portrayed as a victim, as it often happens with film texts dealing with women's issues.

The conflict which emerges is that of Woman versus Society, its mores and customs, and that of Woman against Man. In her earlier films, Sen's focus was always on the failure of marital and heterosexual relationships. Here, she takes the battle to marriage through the theme of friendship. Friendship becomes a key issue in *Iti Mrinalini* through the portrayal of the relationship between Mrinalini and Chintan Nair—a relationship that spans several decades. Perhaps it involves the idea of love, but it is a platonic one. It is almost counterbalanced by the stormy and demanding relationship which Mrinalini shares with Siddhartha. While the latter is selfish and self-absorbed, Chintan comes across as more loving and giving. He is not only supportive and understanding, but also honest with Mrinalini and draws a line somewhere. Chintan is like an oasis in Mrinalini's frenzied and haphazard outer world. There are many questions that this film raises—one of them being about the possibility of there being a pure friendship between a man and a woman, and the other about the various kinds of love in the world at large.

The Idea of Freedom

Yugant

Yugant (1997) is a mature and moving exploration of the lives of Deepak and Anasuya, its two protagonists, and their life together. In the beginning, it seems that their marriage is less than happy because of the onslaught of modernity, but as the film progresses, a network of issues emerges painting a true picture of the reality. As the title suggests, 'yugant' means 'apocalypse' in Bengali, and one finds a certain pessimism pervading the film, regarding Man and his relationship with Nature and that with other human beings in society. This is at the heart of *Yugant* and is explored via the two protagonists of the story.

When the film opens, the estranged couple Deepak and Anasuya meet after a long separation at a small fishing village where they had once honeymooned 17 years ago. Deepak arranges for them to stay at the same guest house too, imaginably in a bid to attempt a reconciliation. When they discover certain objects in the house which have remained there and not been removed over the years, such as a conch shell which they had picked up on one of their walks along the shore, they feel jubilant. However, their erstwhile caretaker is no more—his place now taken by his grandson. Time seems to have moved very fast while the couple's desire is to remain the same—young and ageless perhaps. It is as they confront each other and the past during this trip that they realize that not only have they advanced in years (visible through their physical appearance), but that their natures have also changed invariably.

Illusion and Reality

Right from the very beginning, one gets the sense that Aparna Sen plays on the concept of illusion versus reality, or rather, she plays with the nature of reality itself when, in the course of the narrative, she makes Anasuya dive into a pond during a walk the couple takes in a park. Deepak becomes anxious when she doesn't surface for a while, and when she does, she says that she has been blessed by the folk of the green depths. She tells Deepak that she has become a mermaid. The interaction between the young Deepak and Anasuya is spontaneous, and they are full of love and understanding for each other.

Deepak wants to run away from his family who live in a single, claustrophobic flat in Kalighat, and he and Anasuya perhaps intend to make a better life together when they marry, but when they do get married, they realize that whatever 'love' they might have had in the past now clashes with reality, and life is not all that pleasant. In one of their earlier walks in their carefree days, they are seen to interact without bothering too much about appearances and the ugly nature of the reality surrounding them.

Anasuya is not only playful but also extremely imaginative, which is vindicated by her success in her career as a danseuse. However, keeping the couple's disintegrating marriage at the centre, Sen sets about exploring environmental and other issues as well.

The Changing Environment

Also dotting the narrative are several instances such as the Gulf War, the haunting image of a bird trying to escape the oil spill, the sea no longer being blue-green, the entire environment having changed within a very short span of their lifetime—17 years—which is reflected through their own changed natures. Anasuya, who is an artist with an active imagination, believes that nature speaks to her. She tells Deepak that with the changing times she feels that the 'Sea' also does not speak to her anymore—the very nature of the sea seems to have changed. Sen captures a sense of its beauty through top shots of the white crests of the waves as they hit the shore as well as the blue-green colour of it as Anasuya revels in it. In the end, when the oil spill in the sea catches fire as one of the fishermen throws a lit torch into it, it reflects the polluted nature of it. In its green depths, pollution lurks; appearances can be deceptive, Sen seems to say. The environmental issues explored by Sen—and there are several instances of it throughout the film—also act as a metaphor for the changed relationship between the couple. In fact, it goes on to reflect how the two have changed as individuals too.

Environmental issues come to impinge on their conversation time and again. For instance, the Gulf War, which was aired on television, enter their lives, prompting

Anasuya to adapt her feelings for the poor helpless bird trapped in a sea of oil into a dance drama as only an artist would.

Anasuya, who is an innovative and creative dancer, tries to incorporate the sociopolitical developments around her into her dance dramas, but is stopped short by a local politician who also happens to be a patron of her dance academy, and she is forced to compromise. And yet at one point of time, she would rather forego the birth of her child through an abortion than compromise with her dance and career. Sen does not point accusing fingers at her, nor does she judge her. She simply portrays the drama as it unfolds. The abortion conceivably results in the couple's estrangement. Perhaps that is when Deepak decides to take up a job in Bombay and Anasuya chooses to move to a place near Bhubaneswar to open her dance academy there.

The Indian Woman Coming into Her Own

Most of Sen's film comes to focus on Anasuya and her work. It is her reactions which become the focus of her attention right from the beginning of the film. Sometimes, Sen offers Deepak's reactions as well. From the portrayal of their life together in Calcutta, it becomes clear that Anasuya had to put up with a lot more difficulties than Deepak. When her dancing skills are praised and a New York photojournalist wishes to write about her, Deepak expresses resentment of some sort. Pettiness overcomes him and he even begins to make fun of his wife in front of his colleagues. For the most part, Deepak is portrayed in relation to his colleagues. They are either at a party—there is only one other shot of Deepak at his office—or they are having a get-together at Deepak and Anasuya's house. The fact that Deepak's colleagues are all over the house indicates the fact that Anasuya has very little privacy. They are drunk, and even while the couple are trying to have a serious conversation, one of Deepak's colleagues insists on interrupting them. In fact, Deepak's colleagues' shabby treatment of Anasuya may have contributed to Anasuya feeling trapped in the marriage, and finally leading to the rift between the couple.

Deepak seems to dismiss the fact that his wife's dancing may be as important to her as his job at the advertisement agency is to him. He even asks her sarcastically whether dance is not the only thing which makes up her world. Through such incidents, Sen seems to be underlining the gender inequality which prevails even in educated Bengali households and the Bengali middle class which is usually seen as progressive. Deepak does not seem to mind his colleague Joyeeta's devotion to her work. But when it comes to his own wife, he puts on his best patriarchal self and acts the husband, even preventing her from going on a dance tour to Bangalore when she is pregnant. Anasuya deems it as unforgivable and decides to abort their child, which perhaps leaves Deepak devastated and estranged from her. While he prevents his wife from going to Bangalore, he starts writing a novel about which Anasuya can't help but be critical. This is not to say that she is more artistic than he is, but it is symbolic of the differences between the couple which have already set in.

Most of Sen's films are imbued with autobiographical elements, and *Yugant* is no exception. Aparna Sen's first husband Sanjay Sen worked in an advertising agency, and

Aparna was quite young when she married him. Perhaps the scenes depicted in *Yugant* were experienced by Aparna firsthand. She too was a professional actress and was trying to make a career for herself then. It is not exceptional that a slice of reality found its way into art, and perhaps it is because of this that the film attains a high degree of verisimilitude.

Sen makes it very clear as to what kind of a couple Deepak and Anasuya make. They are an upwardly mobile, middle-class, career-oriented Bengali couple. Although Deepak works at an advertising firm to earn his keep, he is also a singer and a poet at heart. His existential questions dot the narrative, making it quite poetic. In fact, one may venture to say that *Yugant* is perhaps one of Sen's most poetic films. However, in his interactions with his colleagues, he seems quite social and outgoing while Anasuya seems less social and more focused on her career. Most of the shots in the film revolve around her, depicting her as a hardworking, ambitious young woman. But in private, it is Anasuya who is far more spontaneous and fun-loving than Deepak, who seems graver and more serious when the two are alone.

Anasuya seems to be more grounded while Deepak comes across as a more restless soul. He seems to want to escape his present. He does not come across as someone happy with his life. When the two are together, he finds it difficult to accept his wife's success and even expresses resentment at it. This, again, is an example of a relationship marked by a man's inability to sustain it. This is an oft-visited trope in Sen's films and one will encounter several instances of it in this book. In fact, almost all the men in her various narratives fail; it is often a woman who comes to the rescue of another woman.

Deepak, although not overtly patriarchal, makes certain demands on Anasuya which she finds difficult to accept. As she confesses to him later, she did find it difficult to abort their child. While this would hardly be portrayed in a film by a male filmmaker, in Sen's film, it is done in a rather sensitive way. And even if portrayed by a male director, it would be done as an instance of a woman being devoid of womanly attributes and she would be suitably punished for it.

Anasuya shows unusual courage as a woman in single-mindedly pursuing a life which she feels she deserves. By separating from her husband when she feels unfulfilled in marriage, she exercises her agency to enact a certain choice. The film also articulates an evolving Indian society which is, at the same time, opening up to global influences. Therefore, it is not unusual that women will also make choices that are more independent, and forego the traditional roles assigned to them by society. Through such a depiction, Sen's film goes on to pose such questions to her audience, and perhaps the world of Indian cinema is all the richer for it. Where women actors are mostly reduced to secondary and often unimportant roles, Sen's oeuvre is filled with women characters who exercise their choice and their will, thereby opening doorways into other realities.

Deepak's belief that all his problems would be solved through marriage comes to naught, as he realizes later. He suffers from a deep existential angst which is perhaps exacerbated by his extremely successful professional life. He comes to realize that money, success, and such other things mean nothing in the end. Perhaps this is one of the reasons why he can leave his job in the end—as he informs Anasuya on the beach—and maybe even try to lead an uncomplicated life with her.

The End

Yugant has a very interesting ending which is surreal—something which Sen repeats in *15 Park Avenue* as well. Perhaps Deepak's problem, or rather his disillusionment with life, had no suitable solution or ending in reality. Anasuya, through her reaction, almost sends across a message of rejection: she is no longer ready to start afresh with him. The journey which they undertook 17 years ago to start a life together comes full circle at the same spot. He recalls Bhaiyya, his brother-in-law's dedication to his mission of helping displaced local tribal people in Orissa, and him losing his life in the process when local goons kill him, and whose selfless act now makes Deepak's own choices in life much easier and clearer to him. He also fails to accept the fact that changes are inevitable. Where once the sea would communicate with Anasuya as claimed by her, it no longer does so. Deepak fails to understand that it is not only Anasuya who has changed, but perhaps their environment has changed as well.

Through *Yugant*, Aparna Sen not only succeeds in examining contemporary middle-class life but also asks bigger questions such as, what does success mean? What is life? Most of these questions are addressed by Deepak, who does not appear as rooted as examined above. The film goes back and forth in time to weave the story which, besides providing background information, also highlights the different kinds of existences at play. Even though the couple cohabit, their understanding about life is as varied as can be. The film is a bare and honest examination of the crisis in a marital relationship and one can say that it has never been so beautifully portrayed before.

It is a clear exploration of the human, or rather the gendered, predicament of relationships, and how the individual sometimes reveals and more often changes her identity through them. Even though the director's attention is shared between a married couple, one cannot help but note that it is a woman's predicament that is at the centre of the film. It is not surprising given the fact that Sen is a woman film director. What interests her perhaps is the range of human experiences in the evolution of relationships, and this is yet again something that is to be found in almost all her films. In *Yugant*, it is the unhappy maturing of a marriage that is stricken by the frenzied career concerns of modern life.

The couple seem to be greatly in love and share a deep bond in the beginning, but this comes undone through marriage. Is it the institution that Sen is critical of? Is career then an excuse for Deepak and Anasuya to move apart? As always, the man is found wanting. He refuses to grow up or change. Deepak is also not quite expressive and is haunted by memories of loneliness that wracked him as a child. As an adult, he continues to suffer from the same and perhaps demands a great deal of attention from Anasuya. Joyeeta seems to be the other woman in Deepak's life—someone who perhaps gives him a great deal more attention, but is unable to reach his inner being as is made evident from her dull responses to his charged questions on existence, life and others. She is unable to respond to the probing, reflective Deepak and is found wanting.

Even though Anasuya is ideally suited to Deepak and matches his depth, he ends up making a mess of their life together. Instead of letting the marriage evolve on the basis of equality for both partners, he insists on dominating the relationship as is the wont of most Indian men, or so Sen seems to say. Sen then seems to be waging a cultural struggle, as the feminist critic and film scholar Annette Kuhn would say, but through the medium of cinema. One cannot help but posit the question whether, through her cinema, Sen is not trying to argue for social reforms, much like her family members who were once a part of the reforms induced by the Brahmo Samaj.

Arshinagar

As a reader, viewer or critic, one must recognize that adaptation and appropriation are fundamental to the practice, and indeed to the propagation and enjoyment, of literature and the other arts. It is perhaps *Romeo and Juliet* which has the richest stage history. It has been adapted by Hollywood numerous times, closer home by Bollywood in *Qayamat se Qayamat tak* (1988) and *Ram Leela* (2013), and it is no surprise that Aparna Sen—who is known for making films on contemporary sociopolitical issues—based *Arshinagar* (2015) in contemporary times.

Sen's film is an adaptation of Shakespeare's *Romeo and Juliet,* but in a twist of sorts, Sen's hero is a Hindu man while her Juliet is a Muslim woman; herein lies the difference in treatment from other adaptations of the play. The film's scope is thus extended to more than being a mere love story. However, it does not belong to any specific geographical location. The story revolves around squabbles over land involving goons and the underworld. The title—'Arshinagar' or 'the city of mirrors'—speaks of something deep which Sen wants to excavate.

Much like *West Side Story*, Sen's film is also a musical. It contains theatrical props in which books and objects are painted, thus dispensing with realism as we understand it in cinema. Apart from the language and the actors cast, one notices Sen experimenting not only with the contents of the Shakespeare play, but also in terms of the cinematic language. It is a musical with as many as 10 to 12 songs that cover a wide range of genres. She does away with the realistic side of cinema; for one, the Arshinagar in which the story is located is an imaginary place except for the temporal location being specific—contemporary times. The sets of the film are more like theatrical props, as reiterated earlier, which is one of the first things that strike you about the film. The whole of *Arshinagar* has a dream-like quality about it. 'Arshi', which means mirror in Bengali, also wants the viewers to take a good look at themselves, along with the key players in the narrative. One becomes aware of a different cultural form and its context—one which is speaking of a different world. Also, it begins as a tale told to the viewers by Fatima who was once Julekha's ayah and who also acts as the choric character in the film, thus emphasising the theatrical aspect of this narrative and simultaneously calling attention to the fact that it is an adaptation of the Bard's play.

The opening feud is replaced by Fatima's depiction of Arshinagar's locale through a show-and-tell puppet performance at a local *mela*. In several interviews, Sen provides the background to the story. By narrating it as a story, one is at once led to point out the timelessness of such a story and the theatricality of it all. Sen's influence for this film was the 1965 Hollywood musical *West Side Story*, and perhaps her film may even be one of the first musicals in Bengali cinema, considering the way we understand the genre. It is also hailed as the first adaptation of *Romeo and Juliet* in Bengali cinema.

In an interview, Sen said that a nineteenth-century Bengali *Baul*[12] saint Lalon Fakir's song 'Barir kachhe Arshinagar' ('there is a town called Arshinagar near my house'), which speaks of religious tolerance and pluralism, served as the backdrop for her film. In fact, several times the narrative is punctuated by Baul songs which comment on the scenario unfolding in the film.

Julekha's father Sabeer Khan is a construction magnate who is helped in his business by his nephew Tayyeb. While Romeo or Ranajay's father Biswanath Mitra is also in the same business, Ranajay's heart lies in creating music. Time and again, he tells his father that he has no intention of pursuing his father's line of business, leading to a strained relationship between the two.

The families are thus a reflection of each other and the focus, much like Shakespeare's play, is on the trope of neighbourliness which invites hostilities (based on the vested interest of taking over Arshinagar, demolishing the slum, and constructing a mall). Thus, loyalty and distrust that engender the inevitable violence at the beginning of the narrative also aid in some reconciliation in the end. Arshinagar could well stand for contemporary India (a

---

[12]Baul is a mystical folk music tradition from Bengal, combining spiritual philosophy and simple melodies, performed by wandering minstrels who seek divine connection beyond religious boundaries.

theme which Aparna Sen had explored once before in her 2001 film *Mr. and Mrs. Iyer*). Interestingly, she calls *Arshinagar* an extension of that film.

At the heart of the film is Sen's concern for the 'other', which has stoked so much violence and hatred in India in the recent past. Taking a cue from the riots following the demolition of Babri Masjid, Sen says that her primary motivation has been to depict religious intolerance. Perhaps inserting the Baul songs—speaking of love and tolerance—is her way of generating awareness among her audience.

Shakespeare has long been a staple of international performances that interpret his plays in various ways. Closer home, Bollywood also made films based on several of his plays—both comedies as well as tragedies. However, these films—Vishal Bharadwaj being the most famous practitioner of this tradition—render them homegrown products in which the conventions of Bollywood predominate. Fight sequences, melodramatic revenge plots, song-and-dance sequences, and such others are coupled with basic plots from Shakespeare's plays. This, however, is not a recent phenomenon and was a part of Parsi theatre from which they found their way into the film industry. Some of the more popular Shakespeare adaptations are Gulzar's *Angoor* (1982) or even Mansoor Khan's *Qayamat se Qayamat tak* (1988). In later years, of course we had Vishal Bharadwaj's *Maqbool* (2003), *Omkara* (2006) and *Haider* (2014). Critics agree that the perception of Shakespeare as a playwright with particular affinities with mainstream culture facilitated and validated his appropriation in Bollywood.

Critic and academic Paromita Chakravarti asserts that these new, vibrant and unapologetic 'Bollywoodizations' of Shakespeare use the Shakespearean text more as a resource than as the privileged original. This, in turn, represents a vernacular turn which is not only different from, but also runs counter to, the values underlying earlier English language films set in India, like *Shakespeare Wallah* (1965) which reinforced Shakespeare's iconicity and celebrated the high cultural colonial legacy of English theatre.

Aparna Sen's *Arshinagar* can be placed within the body of work that adapts Shakespeare using 'Bollywood conventions' and representational protocol, fusing theatrical events with cinematic modes, and thus effecting radical hybridizations of genres and aesthetics.

Arshinagar may not only be read as a reflection on the larger context of cinematic appropriation of Shakespearean theatre in India, but also as a medium through which Aparna Sen wishes to put across her message of inclusiveness, love and tolerance in society. Roughly based on William Shakespeare's *Romeo and Juliet*, the plot traces the bloody feuds between two warring families—the Khans and the Mitras—who reside in *Arshinagar*. Sen situates her film at a time when there was a sudden surge in real estate dealings, murders, land grabbing, and so on in West Bengal. So she weaves all of that into her plot which gives it a political twinge, as does the fact that her protagonists belong to two different religious denominations which have always been at strife with one another. The film can also be read as a postmodernist re-reading of Shakespeare through cinema.

Arshinagar creates its own aura by borrowing Tollywood's star power. Dev, who is the biggest superstar in the Bengali film industry at the moment, was roped into playing an older Romeo to a very young Juliet. However, Sen's tone in *Arshinagar* was very different from Bengali commercial cinema. This film can thus be seen as a kind of crossover between art-house and commercial cinema, as well as Sen's attempt to reach a wider audience.

Back in the film, Tayyab, Sabeer Khan's nephew, is suspicious and ill-disposed towards the lovers' union. He also manages to injure one of the key members of Mitra's gang. These further distance the two families, setting them on a bloodier, more aggressive and ambitious path where each of the two gang-lords tries to influence the local minister to win him over to his side.

The theatricality of the mise-en-scene which includes a lot of choreographed fight scenes (in the *West Side Story* style) speaks of an experimental cinematic style hitherto not seen in Bengali cinema. It also brings in Brechtian notions of the theatre, such as the demolishing of the fourth wall with the song sequence 'Kaale Paisa wala'. *Arshinagar* can thus be seen as a bold stroke to marry the sister arts of cinema and theatre—creating a unique platform to convey Sen's message.

While it may seem that Sen's film with its rhymed speeches in the vernacular may rob it of its connection with Shakespeare's celebrated play, she is also careful to maintain a link with the Bard. However, she adds a complex layer when she plots the story of young Sabeer Khan's love affair with Madhu (who later becomes a Mitra)—Ranajoy's mother in the distant past—thus bringing in the religious angle. While she was willing to convert to Islam for her love, ultimately they had to abandon their plans to marry because of parental pressure. The young generation, however, in a rather filmi style, wishes to elope, get married and live in Bombay. While Julekha plans to manage the house, Ranajoy plans to earn their keep by performing as a singer.

The markers of religion and identity are important to the delineation of the story, and these are brought out through the costumes. Almost at the beginning of the film when Ranajoy and his friends come to know that the Khan women are going to put up a play, they enter the Khan household clad in *burka*. Julekha mistakenly drags the burka-clad Ranajoy into the bathroom assuming that it is Fati—her ayah. Julekha is dressed as a young man, complete with a turban and a moustache—depicting her as a Hindu. Other instances include Tayyab's gang dressed in black, while Mitra's gang and his house are painted in red. Perhaps they are identity markers related to religion, or perhaps it is an attempt to highlight the theatrical quotient of the film.

However, it is also the vision of a shared and universal humanity as scholar Taarini Mookherjee interprets it in her article.[13] This is also indicative of the fact that externalities are but constructs; as Sen proclaims in her interview to *The Hindu*: underneath, everyone's the same. She also undertakes to tell the tale of subalterns through the various characters inhabiting Arshinagar. While the first few shots establish the key players who belong to the two rich clans, it is only after a while that the other characters who live in the town are seen.

The tea-seller's stall happens to be not only a place of gathering for the townsfolk, but also a point where news is exchanged by all denominations of people. There

---

[13]Mookherjee, Taarini, 'Theorizing the Neighbor: Arshinagar and Romeo and Juliet, Borrowers and Lenders', *The Journal of Shakespeare and Appropriation*, Vol. 12, No. 2, 2019, https://tinyurl.com/2s3vmwv8. Accessed on 12 March 2025.

also seems to be a lot of bonhomie between the various kinds of people as they share tea and gossip. This is also probably the first time in Bengali cinema that the subaltern voice becomes so important, and even though the common people revolt, it is ultimately violence that takes over—stoked by the minister's goons. In an interview with Paromita Chakravarti, Sen stated that she used the Baul figure to depict the central motif of her film: 'the two opposite sides of human nature, one that is able to love and the other only hates. Basically, showing love as a counterpoint to hate.'

The other central concern in the film is *porshi*—another idea she borrows from Lalon Fakir's 'Arshinagar'. The word 'porshi' means 'neighbour' or 'the one next to you', but Lalon extends its meaning to explore profound spiritual and human connections.

In *Arshinagar*, the porshi represents the 'other'—someone who seems distant or different but is revealed to be a reflection of oneself upon deeper understanding. Lalon challenges the boundaries we create between the 'self' and the 'other', urging individuals to look beyond physical and social divisions to recognize the shared humanity and divinity that bind us together.

Although Aparna Sen can be read as a feminist filmmaker, one can see that in the latter part of her career, she moved on to subjects that do not deal only with women's issues; instead, her films come to adopt a political hue, almost acting as mouthpieces for the way she views society. Sen's motivation to make the film as one that depicts communal strife is borne out through the way she views society and the way she introduces the main characters of the drama, as well as the plot, costume design, and the idea of the common man and woman's grouse against land grabbing. She states, 'Land grab is something I have been very interested in ever since Singur and Nandigram [sites of people's movements against the state land acquisition]. Then also the way in which the Gujarat riots were fanned by distributing petrol to the rioters. The way the fire brigade and the police were not allowed to be called until some hours had passed. And this was largely the work of politicians to further their ends.' All these are woven into the plot in a minimalist way. The state machinery comes to be represented through the minister along with his two henchmen who not only aid in stoking the fire which burns the local temple down, but also help in stirring up communal riots. Time and again, contemporary political events find their way into Sen's films, making them urgent and interesting.

The film traverses a different kind of path, at least in the Bengali film industry, as it takes recourse to theatre, cinema and music, and becomes a successful admixture of all three. While the basic plot remains that of *Romeo and Juliet*, other aspects come to attain much more importance.

Ghawre Bairey Aaj

Aparna Sen's *Ghawre Bairey Aaj* (2019) is a contemporary rendition of Rabindranath Tagore's 1915 novel *Ghare Baire*. It is the story of two friends—Nikhilesh and Sandip—with widely differing worldviews and ideologies. Nikhilesh's wife Bimala falls in love with his best friend Sandip when Nikhilesh brings her out of seclusion. Sandip appears more attractive to Bimala because of his fiery radicalism. A fallout occurs between the two friends because of this.

Sandip's preaching of Swadeshi ideals brings about chaos in Nikhilesh's *zamindari*, which ends tragically in his death and Bimala's untimely widowhood.

Aparna Sen's *Ghawre Baire Aaj* follows the basic plot of Tagore's novel, but this time, Nikhilesh is the editor of an online news portal called *India Online*, Sandip a Hindu nationalist and historian, and Bimla a Dalit orphan girl. She is adopted by Nikhilesh's parents and renamed Brinda in keeping with their upper-class status, given an education in a private boarding school and then a top elite institution in Delhi, and married to Nikhilesh.

Sen introduces certain key issues such as casteism, the current political situation in India, adultery and friendship, which run as motifs throughout the length of her narrative. While her opinions on women's issues, environmental degradation and religion in politics are reflected in films such as *Parama, Paromitar Ek Din, Yuganta, Mr. and Mrs. Iyer* and *Goynar Baksho*, this film is probably one of her most urgent commentaries on the times.

The film begins in the present with Bimla (the name with which she was born to tribal parents in Jharia, Bihar) telling her side of the story (much in the same way as Tagore's novel which is structured in the form of diary entries), and laying the foundation of the story. She comes across as a dutiful wife to Nikhilesh who is much older than her. As the narrative moves forward, one is also introduced to the finer details of their life together. She is a graduate of Lady Shri Ram College, an elite and premier institution in the nation's capital, and now works as a proofreader for Oxford University Press.

Sandip, his best friend, arrives in the capital to take up the position of a visiting lecturer at a university. Sandip is a sympathizer of right-wing politics and comes across as an opportunist who wants to further his end alongside that of his party.

When the film opens, Nikhilesh is preoccupied with the building of a hospital for adivasis in Bastar. It is a disputed piece of land which earlier housed a religious building. This brings him into direct conflict with Sandip whom he calls his political adversary and who finally turns into his nemesis. While Sandip decides to stay at his friend's place for old times' sake, his party members are not too happy with the arrangement as it may tarnish their image and defeat their purpose of gathering support for their cause, and honouring Sandip for his activities.

It is inevitable that a comparison with Satyajit Ray's *Ghare Baire* (1984) would perhaps unwittingly creep in. In contrast to Ray's Sandip who appears greedy for luxuries such as foreign cigarettes and travelling in first-class railway compartments, Sen's Sandip—played by Jisshu Sengupta—appears far more diabolical, but is physically much more charming. He is also orthodox but smoothly goes about seducing Brinda.

On the first day, the two friends visit various old places from their past college life where they reminisce about many past events and shared memories, and Sandip's strident advocacy of Hindutva ideals is revealed. A past incident of protest at the university reveals Nikhilesh to be someone who is open to dialogues, aiding in the mitigation of difficulties and issues. Sandip, however, comes across as violence-loving and radical. Even as an adult, Nikhilesh retains much of the gentleness of his youth. He also comes across as more liberal when he marries the Dalit girl Brinda and gives her a name and a comfortable home. While Sandip chooses to see it as a move that tries to establish the point that Nikhil is liberal, the latter defends his position calmly and, in a noncommittal way, stresses on her achievements. However, his dream project of the hospital takes him away from home and his beloved wife quite often, leaving the field wide open for Sandip to make his move.

Adultery

It is only at this point that Sen interjects with an interesting angle to the story—that of adultery—which was visited by Sen elsewhere, namely in her 1984 film *Parama*, but only in an oblique manner, and to a certain extent in *Iti Mrinalini*. However, in this film, it comes to occupy a central place. Sandip is deeply attracted to Brinda—his conquests of women have been many, and his conquest of his best friend's wife would no doubt create issues, but eros, or rather lust, takes the driver's seat here. He goes on to talk about love and adultery, and in the same breath, he talks about Krishna's longing for Radha. What we find is that Brinda gets into a physical relationship with Sandip and the two go on to spend a lot of time with each other, to the extent that she also begins to change herself with visits to temples (Nikhilesh is an atheist), and wears sarees where once the *salwar kameez* was her favourite outfit.

Brinda is attracted to Sandip for several reasons; for one, he comes across as a seasoned speaker who puts across his ideas much more assertively than Nikhilesh does. Secondly and more importantly, he spends a lot of time with Brinda on the pretext of looking at Delhi afresh with her eyes, and there are several shots of them visiting various parts of the city. Nikhilesh, as Sen draws him up in the film, is no longer young. Moreover, there is quite a huge age difference between the couple which leaves Brinda quite dissatisfied when it comes to their conjugal life. Nikhilesh is also ailing with severe health issues, while Sandip keeps himself fit. The three-month interlude in which Nikhilesh leaves the station to observe subaltern life in Bastar brings Sandip and Brinda closer. On his sudden return from Bastar, Brinda finds it difficult to hide her feelings for Sandip and begins to resent Nikhilesh's presence.

An estrangement between the couple results in Brinda hiding from Nikhilesh the fact that she is pregnant with Sandip's child. When Sandip refuses to accept her citing the fact that her lower-caste status would not suit his brand of politics and asks her to abort the child, she finally comes to understand his real nature. She is also privy to the fact that while Sandip ostensibly professes unity, he also displays his hypocritical stance in letting his protegé Amulya's Muslim friend Junaid die. Sandip's callous attitude awakens her to reality and she now turns to Nikhilesh. She confesses everything to him, and not unsurprisingly, he finds it difficult to accept it at first, but soon reconciles himself to it and decides to bring up the child as his own.

Of Men and Failed Relationships

As in her other films, here too, Sen's focus is on the issue of failed relationships. Her focus is on the heterosexual ones in which the man inevitably fails the woman. In Brinda's case, both Nikhilesh and Sandip fail her. Having been brought up as a girl in the upper echelons of society, she is told by her *dadi* or grandmother that she wouldn't be accepted in the upper-class, upper-caste society despite her education because of her low caste, and no one in the village could be a suitable companion to her either because she has an English education. Nikhilesh then decides to undo the injustice and marries her, though he finds it difficult to answer Sandip's very sharp questions about his actual motives in doing so.

Sen's film branches off into many concerns unlike Ray's, which was a faithful adaptation of Tagore's novel, and in which Ray made Bimala's voice the central one. There is, however, no angle provided by Aparna as to why Brinda marries the much older Nikhilesh. It is not that she could not have been acquainted with other young men, having attended an elite college or meeting a few in her line of work. And if she were indeed in love with her husband in a relatively new marriage—both claim that it is only three years old—she could not have been tempted into a relationship with Sandip when Nikhil had already told her about Sandip's various past relationships with other women.

Perhaps Sen chooses not to dwell on the subject. Brinda ceases to be of interest as either a woman or a Dalit person early on in the film. For instance, quite cryptically, she does not even reiterate the fact once—even when she introduces herself—that she was born in Jharia to parents who worked in a coal mine and whose deaths brought her to Delhi, to the place where her grandmother worked. It is the men who contemplate about it, especially Sandip who thinks that Nikhilesh may have married the poor Dalit girl out of pity for her or because he wanted to make a point about how liberal he was.

Sandip, on one hand, for all his rhetoric about serving the nation, love, and so on, refuses to take any responsibility for his actions when he impregnates Brinda. For him, it is nothing more than a fling, or better still, just another conquest. He casually boasts to Nikhilesh, his oldest friend, 'I don't know how many bastards I may have accidentally fathered,' which neither of them finds insensitive or callous.

They find other concerns much more pressing, for example, nationalism—for which the friends have differing feelings and definitions. This is one of the reasons why Sen's adaptation of Tagore's novel perhaps becomes relevant and even timely. Politics occupies a seminal place in this film. But this is not one of the main reasons why the friends have a fallout, even though Nikhilesh worries about it and calls Sandip his political adversary. Instead, it is Sandip's thoughtless affair with Brinda which wounds Nikhilesh deeply. Although they are childhood friends and refer to each other as the oldest friend they have, Sandip's thoughtless action has implications for more than one life—it destroys Nikhilesh utterly. Sandip cites it as a suicidal move for his political career. When his party approaches him to nominate him as a Rajya Sabha member, it comes with the addendum that he show Nikhilesh his place and ask him to back out of his hospital project on the disputed plot of land.

Although all of Aparna Sen's films are imbued in politics of various kinds, *Ghawre Baire Aaj* is perhaps the only one where she expresses her political stance so very openly and boldly. In an interview, Sen stated that it expressed disillusionment not only with the Right but also with any kind of fundamentalism.

In fact, even the extreme Left or Maoism is critiqued in this film when Sandip expresses his disenchantment with it. As a young man, Sandip had confessed to Nikhil that he had joined the Maoists but their extremist ways and what he calls 'total obedience' to the orders of their superiors without questioning their actions caused him to be disillusioned with the movement. Furthermore, having to murder another human being—who was branded an informer—disgusted him so much that he had to appeal to the state via his grandfather to rescue him from the Maoists and allow him to come back home. It was this experience which prompted him to become a nationalist. However, even though Sen tries to problematize both the political viewpoints, her bias is made quite evident when Professor Mitra talks at length about the Hindu religion and admonishes Nikhilesh for reducing it to a black-and-white thing.

The secular side also fails to appear entirely convincing as Nikhilesh, though forgiving to a fault, remains notably silent about his own beliefs. He also comes across as an anglophile with a heavy accent, pipe-smoking ways and conversations with colleagues and friends which are mostly conducted in English.

Neither Tagore's nor Ray's Nikhilesh came across as an anglophile. If anything at all, he came across as a covert Swadeshi and someone who has his subjects' welfare at heart. Aparna's Nikhilesh, on the other hand, appears stunned when he confronts the reality of adivasi life in Bastar. What begins as the project of an armchair socialist (which is what Sandip calls him) sitting in his New Delhi office becomes a serious effort only by the end of the film when he decides to spend three months in Bastar documenting Shweta Devi's activities and Dr Binayak Sen's work among the adivasis. But by then, it is too late as he succumbs to an assassin's bullets as he comes home one night from protests about the killing of the Muslim youth Junaid. With protests becoming the order of the day with ordinary citizens playing active roles in them, Sen decided to portray one such protest in her film with Nikhil's friends and colleagues participating quite actively in it—even organizing it.

The Right and Left brands of politics are quite explicitly dealt with in the film. Where Ray's Sandip only managed to appear greedy—a crazy glint in his eyes on beholding the gold *mohurs*—Sen's appears outright villainous. He not only manipulates Brinda but also chastises her for even suggesting that they live together as man and wife, the reason being her caste. For much like Nikhil, Sandip too, despite his professed work in the gram panchayat of his village in Bihar's Chhapra district, refuses to let go of his traditional values that profess a strict caste hierarchy. Whereas Tagore's and Ray's Sandip admitted defeat and left Nikhilesh's estate Sukhshayor, Sen's Sandip refuses to give in and brands Nikhil a Maoist sympathizer to the media and calls his death the handiwork of Maoists in order to further his as well as his party's goals and absolve them of the crime.

In this case too, Brinda had every right not to indulge in a passionate affair with Sandip. In the twenty-first century, when women have much more freedom than what they possibly had, say, in the nineteenth century, it is impossible to think that Brinda could not have met any other man apart from Nikhilesh. These are some of the questions one is left wondering about at the end of the film. How then does Aparna Sen negotiate her stand vis-à-vis feminism? How does she account for the fact that the two men in the film have definitive career paths and goals, while Brinda is reduced to almost a housewife-like position? She has no great career to boast of apart from that of being a proofreader who works from home for Oxford University Press. Also, when Sandip enquires about Nikhilesh's sudden decision to marry Brinda, the two friends talk about her either as a victim of societal mores and measures, or in terms of her physical attractiveness. The fact that she is a human being and, more importantly, a woman who may have an identity of her own, somehow manages to escape them.

The friendship between the two men is destroyed because of Brinda and not political differences as Nikhilesh suspected. Even though the two had different worldviews, their friendship was the bond that prompted Nikhilesh to let Sandip stay at his place. It seems that Sandip had known no other friend except Nikhilesh. However, their college friend Sammy's continuing friendship with Nikhilesh offsets the selfish one that Sandip represents. It remains the same because they seem to share the same ideologies.

It is perhaps with the etching of this new-age Bimala's character that Sen's film takes on a bold stance, marking a point of departure from both Ray's and Tagore's versions. While Tagore's and Ray's Bimala could only act as a passive victim of Sandip's schemes and Nikhilesh's death, Aparna Sen's Brinda takes a pistol and shoots the demagogue Sandip. But one wonders whether that is really a feasible solution. In Sen's oeuvre, Brinda perhaps takes the boldest stance in shooting her oppressor. But one is left wondering as to whether or not Sandip is the real enemy. Or does the malaise run much deeper?

Does her subaltern instinct (despite what Sandip terms as the 'Brahminization' of her tribal identity) of protesting against her oppressor suddenly rear its head? Is Brinda finally able to take revenge for all the other Bimalas taken advantage of by the Sandips of the world? Although this is a bold move, one wonders what the director hopes to achieve with such an ending. If one lays the entire blame at Sandip's feet, one is left with the feeling that Bimala or Brinda has no agency. Both Tagore's and Ray's heroines exercised their will and not their judgement in getting involved with Sandip. The other choice was simply not to get involved, however great the temptation may have been.

A Room of Her Own

15 Park Avenue

Sen's *15 Park Avenue* (2005) is centred around Meethi who has been diagnosed with schizophrenia. And it is her inner world that Sen comes to explore in this film. As in films dealing with differently abled characters, Sen invites her audience to ponder over the categories of normal/abnormal and reality/irreality. The film begins with a woman named Meethi being driven to the address '15 Park Avenue' by her elder sister. However, after an exasperating search for the house at the given address, Meethi's sister Annu (played by Shabana Azmi) loses her cool and decides to go back home. There is no road by that name, and it is this intriguing address and the search for home that the narrative focuses on.

The world considers Meethi 'crazy', and the beggar woman at their gate also gazes at her familiarly as if the two belong to the same world. As the narrative moves forward, one realizes that there are many temporal registers to the film. It, however, begins in the present, narrating Meethi's crisis aggravated by a sister who is devoted to her but loses her cool quite often. Her mother also gets a *shaman* (spiritual healer) to try and cure her of her disease, or in their parlance, get rid of the spirits tormenting her. Meethi's caregiver, otherwise a caring person, is nevertheless an uneducated woman. She is oblivious to the prophylaxis of mental illness and treats Meethi whichever way she deems fit.

One of the main characters in the film aside from Meethi is her elder sister Annu. She is a constant fixture beside Meethi. Interestingly, there are three perspectives from which Annu is seen in the film. The first is that of Meethi, who feels that her sister has changed and is scarier now because she gets angry quite often. The second is that of Sanjeev, Annu's friend and lover from Presidency College, who, having been invited to Princeton University for a term, wants her to come along. Annu, who takes her responsibility towards Meethi quite seriously, keeps putting off the decision to accompany him. The third perspective is that of Dr Kunal Barua, Meethi's psychiatrist, who discusses her case with Annu and the two are often thrown together, developing a friendship.

Apart from Annu, there is really no one else willing to shoulder Meethi's responsibility which is a heavy burden. Mahesh, Annu's younger brother, lives elsewhere with his own family consisting of a wife and three children. In fact, he doesn't even take care of their mother. He comes over for tea and to introduce his newborn daughter to them, and tries to indulge Meethi in an offhand way. In fact, his whole family treats Meethi as if she is mad and shows her no sympathy whatsoever.

In *Paromitar Ek Din* (2000) too, Khuku, who has schizophrenia, is treated as crazy and is often called so.

The subtle nuances among various types of mental illnesses are never examined in the films. Sen merely represents the terms by which people think about mental illnesses. One wonders if the director also does not think of it the same way. Sen's films are imbued with a personal touch which problematizes the artist's distance from her works. So in *15 Park Avenue,* too, the treatment of Meethi's character is along the same lines as Khuku's. Meethi's mother also treats her like that. Annu, though protective, is not necessarily sympathetic to Meethi all the time.

Annu, who is an academic, also writes books and articles which require a certain degree of focus and concentration. She mostly finds time for herself at night when the rest of the household is sleeping. It is at this moment that she finds her attention diverted by Meethi's antics which irritate her a great deal, but when Meethi's handler Charu scolds her for them, Annu tries to pacify her.

Annu comes across as a rather selfless being because she gave up a lot of things that mean a lot to her, such as her own family, companionship, love, and so on. It is only in the second half of the film, during the Bhutan trip, that she tries to relate to Meethi and takes it upon herself to find *15 Park Avenue* as a mission because it means so much to Meethi. Annu comes across as more motherly and responsible towards Meethi than her own mother. She regularly meets Dr Barua to discuss Meethi's condition. It is through their interactions that we come to know about Meethi's ailment and its background. Annu, who comes across as lonely, also finds a companionable shoulder in Kunal Barua.

Annu's account of Meethi's illness stretches as far back as her childhood when she found Meethi preoccupied with her own world, shying away from interacting with other children. When the psychiatrist asks Annu if there were other manifestations of the disease, she finds it difficult to believe that there was something wrong with Meethi. It is not clear from all the above as to when Meethi was diagnosed with schizophrenia.

15 Park Avenue is an example of the inability of educated upper-class Indians to understand the needs of a person with mental disability. Meethi's father is a brigadier in the army; her mother cannot seem to be bothered with her. Annu takes it upon herself to take care of Meethi. This is strange given that the former is her stepsister. Throughout the narrative, Meethi can be seen with Annu most of the time.

The film can be neatly divided into two phases. In the first half, Meethi's life revolves around Annu's, and vice versa. Meethi is mostly seen from Annu's perspective. She tries to include Meethi in her daily activities and even in family activities, such as meeting and holding Mahesh's new baby as well as sitting and chatting with them. Annu seems like a crusader for Meethi. Besides her career, her only other focus seems to be Meethi and her wellbeing. She also refers to Meethi as her child because she is almost 18 years younger than her. Even though Annu has appointed a caregiver for her, she still sends her to a daycare so that she can be looked after properly. While her personal life suffers, she cannot commit to going away to the US with Sanjeev; her work is the only other life that she leads peacefully.

One night, Annu is particularly short with Meethi and questions her version of reality. In Meethi's world, she shares a joint bank account with her husband Jojo, and when Annu corrects her, she gets angry and questions Annu's version of reality. What if Annu was not really a professor of physics but was only imagining it? Sen perhaps wants us to view the world of the 'other' (in this case Meethi) sympathetically. It is almost philosophical in that even in our own Indian philosophical system, Adi Shankaracharya preaches that reality is nothing more than an illusion. So the question is: whose world is more real? The one which Annu and the others inhabit, or the other to which Meethi disappears at the end of the narrative?

It is almost an hour into the film when the director introduces us to Meethi's imagined husband 'Jojo'. Joydeep Roy is visiting Bhutan with his family consisting of his wife and two young children Joyeeta and Jishnu. When he sees Meethi near a riverbank, old memories come rushing back. The perspective shifts entirely to his consciousness—his thoughts about Meethi. Even though in abandoning Meethi, he comes across as a failure at the end, Sen, for the first time, allows the man to present his perspective to the viewers.

Jojo complains of Annu's domineering attitude. The latter tried to warn Jojo that Meethi, not being 'normal' like the rest of them, would not be able to handle a relationship like marriage which was demanding. However, as he claims, he was not detracted by the prospect of a less-than-normal wife and got engaged to Meethi. He once again notes Annu's strong opposition to this. The parents seemed ineffectual in expressing themselves and went along with Annu. Is it because they found her mature, responsible and worldly-wise? Jojo makes a rather insensitive comment about Annu—citing her dominating nature as the cause for her divorce. Later, he deserts Meethi for having been gang-raped while on duty at a border town, reporting on post-poll violence.

While Annu tries to decipher whether or not the disease was triggered by the rape, one begins to wonder why such questions were not raised by anyone before.

The Failure of the Men

When Kunal Barua begins investigating Meethi's case (it seems that Dr Ahmed, her previous doctor, had paid very little attention to her needs), the viewers also get full details of it. Along with her parents who found it difficult to manage Meethi, her older brother Mahesh also saw it fit for her to be put away in an institution. It is only Annu who thinks that it would be inhuman and that Meethi deserves to be home like the rest of them.

Mahesh is rarely seen with Meethi. In fact, he sides with his wife Padma and shows little kindness towards Meethi when his children mock her story about having five children. While they amuse themselves at her expense, Mahesh makes no effort to scold or reprimand them for their poor behaviour. Padma—who has arrived with her family to show off her newborn daughter—is also anything but kind to Meethi. The entire family treats her as though she were a stranger or a madwoman, showing little regard for her as a fellow human being. Despite being aware of her illness and considering themselves educated, they exhibit a complete lack of compassion towards her. Perhaps to highlight the fact that Annu is the person who does the actual looking-after, Sen gives more screen time to her. Alongside Meethi's life, it is also that of Annu which gets highlighted in the film. Whereas Sen tries to bring out the inner life of Meethi with her oft-reported stories of her baby 'Ayesha', her five children, and husband Jojo, and their new home at 15 Park Avenue, Annu's external life is also portrayed in the film.

Sen also seems to be making a point that so-called intellectual people like Annu seem to lack the imagination or even the ability to see other worlds. Forever stuck in her intellectual life, she fails to appreciate the 'other'. Although it must be said to Annu's credit that she is much more sympathetic to Meethi than even her own mother. Annu seems to have put her own life on hold because she feels that Meethi needs her, while Sanjeev, her lover, wants her to be put in institutionalized care. He doesn't seem to have a family, is in love with Annu, and apart from a career as a professor, seems to have no other care in the world. He comes across as ambitious; when Princeton University invites him as a visiting professor for a year, he accepts the offer. He also wants to indulge in some travelling and have a good time with Annu. In the end, just like Jojo who left Meethi, Sanjeev also abandons Annu. He decides to push forward his visit to the US and break up with Annu.

Jojo is completely thrown off balance when he comes to know that his life has a parallel existence in someone else's life—as Meethi's husband Jojo. But he decides to keep Meethi company despite his wife's disapproval. This is rather insensitive and selfish on his part, since he brought his family to Bhutan on a vacation. Instead of that, he ends up spending a lot of time with Meethi. Jojo seems to be suddenly overcome by guilt and feelings of sadness for Meethi, which do not ring true. Perhaps this is what Sen tries to highlight yet again in this film, namely that a woman's relationship with a man does not yield anything of value, but can only result in hurt and unhappiness.

Jojo goes so far as to tell Annu that Meethi does not trust her, but instead looks to him for help in finding 15 Park Avenue. It is almost as if he is amused or curious about the turn of events in Meethi's life. As he tells his wife (in a voice-over), he still cannot relate to Meethi and that nothing has changed since the last time that he saw her. One wonders why this sudden surge of interest in Meethi then? While Dr Barua thinks it may even help Meethi relate to another human being, Annu remains as sceptical as ever. She is less than trusting of Jojo, but has no choice but to go along with the others since they seem to think that it is a good idea.

In all, the men in this narrative do not come off looking too good. Kunal Barua, Meethi's doctor, seems to be the only person who is painted in a positive light. He seems to get involved in Meethi's case, though he keeps telling Annu that she cannot be cured. One wonders whether he can be seen as a foil to Sanjeev along with the other men in the narrative—someone who is there to look after not only Meethi, but perhaps also Annu, who seems to lack a shoulder to cry on.

Goynar Baksho

The story of *Goynar Baksho* (2013) begins in 1949, two years after India got independence, when a young girl named Somlata gets married and moves into her in-laws' palatial house in rural West Bengal. She is married into a family of erstwhile *zamindar*s (feudal lords) from Faridpur in East Bengal, who have been left with nearly nothing in the wake of the Partition. The men in the family would rather while away their time fishing, fighting lawsuits against each other, and visiting courtesans. However, at the centre of the story is a ghost of a female relative of her husband—'Pishima'—who, while dead, is a feisty woman and manages to keep her place in the family by sheer grit and through material valuables in the form of a box of precious jewellery.

Goynar Baksho is an adaptation of the celebrated Bengali writer Shirshendu Mukhopadhyay's novel *Rashmonir Shonadana*. Even though it lacks drama, it is perhaps one of the strongest films in Aparna Sen's repertoire in terms of its feminist ideals. At the heart of the story are three strong women from three separate generations, bound together by a box of jewellery. And all three of them put it to great use. Rashmoni or Pishima uses it to make a place for herself in her paternal family as her living relatives are all waiting to snatch it away once she dies. Later in the narrative, prompted by Pishima's ghost, Somlata pawns a piece of jewellery to establish a saree-trading business with her husband. In contrast, her daughter Chaitali, belonging to a different generation, views jewellery with disdain and gives it away to her lover, a *muktijoddha* (freedom fighter) fighting for the liberation of Bangladesh. It is a poignant tale told most humorously onscreen. However, Sen wrought several changes to the novel to give shape to her particular vision.

The film spans two time periods: the first focuses on Somlata's life and experiences within the household, while the second shifts to a later era when her daughter Chaitali has grown up and started attending college, as depicted in the latter part of the film. The film does not venture to tell us about post-Independence Bengali society in India, but instead chooses to focus on Somlata's daily activities and her transition from a housewife to a successful entrepreneur. However, it does satirize the men of her family in no uncertain terms—painting them as greedy, villainous good-for-nothings. Through several dialogues, sequences, characterization and sundry other devices, Sen makes it evident to her audience that the men are nothing short of failures. They would rather sell everything of value in the family for money and their daily upkeep than go out to work. Chandan, Somlata's husband, is the only man who finds redemption in the hands of the director as he sets out to restore the lost glory of the family and earn money as guided by his wife.

Time and again, Sen has pointed out the failure of heterosexual relationships and women expressing helplessness in the face of patriarchal oppression and violence. *Goynar Baksho* is no exception to that. Somlata's father-in-law would rather spend money on the upkeep of a mistress called Chameli, as was the wont of the zamindars, than lend money to his younger son for his business. He also insults Somlata quite often because she belongs to a poor family. He doesn't listen to his wife and distrusts everybody when it comes to money.

The eldest son is a gambler and indulges in fishing with his younger brother day after day, rather than work. Even though the matriarch of the family finds it disgusting, she also finds it difficult to express her annoyance. When Chandan sets up the saree shop in the new market in town, his older brother connives with his father to learn about the whereabouts of the capital with which he has set up the shop. On learning that Somlata helped Chandan with the capital, he becomes furious and sets about insulting her in front of the others. He only stops when Pishima's ghost threatens to expose the truth about him.

Unlike other commercial Bengali films of recent times which use songs in imitation of Hindi cinema, Sen simply refuses to use them. But she does use music in interesting ways in certain sequences. Instead of making the scene of Somlata's interrogation (by her father-in-law) a straightforward q-and-a session, the director introduces music and makes the principal characters speak in rhyme. The whole sequence has great comic appeal, but nonetheless succeeds in driving home the point. Even when goaded on by Pishima's ghost to reveal the truth about her father-in-law in public, Somlata desists, firmly stands her ground, and proves her good upbringing even though her family lacks in money and does not belong to the zamindar class—of which her father-in-law constantly reminds her.

Unequal friendships and female camaraderie are a few of the major tropes in this story. Pishima, for some reason, takes to this young and naïve daughter-in-law of the family, and when she gives up the ghost with a sigh, she looks to Somlata for help with her jewellery box. However, she remains merely the custodian of the box, making Somlata promise that she would never wear even one of the pieces; she makes Somlata hide the box at great risk to herself. The other relatives hunt around the house looking for the baubles, but whenever they are within sprinting distance of the box, Pishima's ghost comes to the rescue and saves the day. Pishima seems to be the only friend Somlata has in the house. She is hardly seen to engage with anyone else in the household. Divided by strife, yet united by the game of chess, the draw of the hookah, and the need to save money, the two elderly patriarchs of the two families spend time with each other, but the women are forbidden to interact with each other.

The past keeps interjecting at various levels—the loss of a happy married life, and in case of Somlata's in-laws, the lament about having to leave behind their land and zamindari, their only source of income. The tenuous symbols of the past—in the form of stone fairies, antique furniture and crystal chandeliers—are slowly sold off or pawned to get money for fighting lawsuits, rather than their own subsistence. While the men lament or are indifferent (especially Chandan and his elder brother), they do nothing to keep the family honour intact. It is the women who feel their loss more acutely, and thus Somlata sets about trying to earn their upkeep, goaded on by Pishima or rather her ghost, who does not hesitate to call her nephew useless.

At a time when women of her class in society were not even allowed to express their opinions no matter what the men did, the fact that Somlata decides to venture out and run a business sets her apart from the other women in her family. While the latter remain engaged in gossiping, household chores, and looking after their many children and family, Somlata does not even think of having children, setting about making a 'man' of her husband instead. Her appearance is that of a timid woman who stutters whenever she is nervous (a trait which mysteriously disappears after her daughter grows up and she becomes the matriarch); she is gentle but possesses courage and wit. She is the hero of this story.

Three generations and the way a box of jewellery changes in significance with time are what *Goynar Baksho* is all about. While it meant security in the case of Rashmoni, to Somlata this very same box becomes capital, and to Chaitali, it is a means of doing something meaningful for people fighting for their motherland.

Widowed at the tender age of 12, Pishima remained a deprived soul most of her life. While Sen does not dwell too much upon the brutal conditions under which widows lived, a few shots of the young Rashmoni shorn of her long and gorgeous hair suffice, as does the sequence of her approaching Ramkhilan, the manservant, for quenching her sexual thirst. This is also instrumental in showing her resourcefulness in getting what she wants. And this is a characteristic that she possesses even after death, when she rescues her jewellery box from the other members of the family. In her interactions with Somlata at various points of time, Pishima reveals the story of her sad and deprived life to the latter—a very strong aspect of sexuality, desires and wants lingering in the background and in their exchanges.

Oppression and Emancipation

This trope—a recurring one in Aparna Sen's films—takes on a special hue here when the condition of three generations of women is portrayed, inviting comparison on the part of the discerning viewer and critic. In British India, the year 1856 saw the abolition of the prohibition against widow remarriages; however, even after the law was enacted, violence and social ostracism against widows and their second husbands were customary. Orthodox customs conveniently retained the virtuousness of the sacred texts inscribed on the woman's body, deterring every possible form of autonomy encouraged by legal reforms.

This cultural and political history can be mapped through the character of Pishima and the incidents marking her life, which begin more or less from the late nineteenth century. Her witty rebuttals from the beginning of the film bring to light the dietary and other restrictions imposed on widows. In retaliation, when she becomes a ghost, she tricks and confuses Somlata into putting salt in the mutton dish thrice while declaring that she will not be eating the dish as she must follow the norms accorded to her as a *bidhabā* (widow), even though she is a ghost.

Sen introduces female desire through the figure of the widow. Pishima exercises a certain kind of autonomy in the absence of a husband, and eggs Somlata on to have an affair with Rafique—comparing a husband to everyday wear and lovers to exotic and expensive sarees. Through Somlata, Pishima perhaps wants to voyeuristically enjoy the consummation of sexual desires which have remained unfulfilled in her own life. The film visualizes this through Rashmoni's attraction towards Ramkhilaon, and here Aparna Sen is quite explicit via her camera. It is a physical hunger that Rashmoni feels for Ramkhilaon's body. She flirts, her gaze unwavering (possibly because she exercises a certain kind of power: that of being the master's daughter and an upper-caste woman, but also as a beautiful woman), and she is shown to be comfortable with her sexuality. However, in the flogging and subsequent murder of Ramkhilaon, we painfully recognize that defiance entails tragedy. And when Pishima (as a ghost) solicits a vivid description of Somlata's sexual relationship, we also realize the profound sexual deprivation experienced by child widows.

Normative codes were further safeguarded by rendering

the widow financially vulnerable, and it is on this point that *Goynar Baksho* departs from the norm. The jewellery box is emblematic of security and Rashmoni is not only aware of its value, but also utilizes it to retain her position in her family whom she refers to as a brood of vultures. The list of gold ornaments is preserved even after her demise, as we see Somlata hand it over to Chaitali for further safekeeping. Throughout the narrative, the box keeps coming to the rescue of these women.

The Box

The jewellery box is an important motif in *Goynar Baksho*. For Pishima, the jewellery comes to symbolize wealth. And as Sen says in one of her interviews, for Somlata, it becomes capital. As Aparna admits, this is what women in those times did. Somlata is as clever as Rashmoni, '...negotiating a space for herself in the male-dominated household and society. Timid outwardly with a stutter (I really wanted to introduce this human element in her character), Somlata turns out to be the force behind the family, gradually pulling it out of the ruin that the men pushed it into, with their debauchery that extends to heaping riches on their mistresses.'

Somlata's timid and stammering demeanour, coupled with an entrepreneurial temperament and a non-greedy nature, make her the ideal candidate for the safekeeping of the jewellery box. It also provides her with the necessary apparatus to capitalize on her intellect. In passing the jewellery box to Somlata, Pishima provides her with the economic independence unavailable to her by virtue of her class position (with the exception of her husband, the men in the family are totally against the business and the establishment of a shop, and speak rather derisively about it). Fuelled by gratitude as well as a kind of empathy that she feels for Rashmoni, Somlata decides to name the shop after Pishima, which fills the latter with happiness and a new purpose of being.

Immediately after this, we see Rashmoni's ghost beginning to keep tabs on the sales, along with helping Somlata procure a wider variety of sarees from all over the country by night. Somlata thus spearheads this desire to be economically self-sufficient hitherto denied to Pishima and the former generation of women and widows.

The Rose

Even though ambiguous (we merely get oblique hints via roses placed at her doorstep and one lone conversation), Somlata's relationship with the poet Rafique is one of yearning and transgression. When Pishima implores her to transcend the binaries of sin and virtue, it functions as another way for her to gain agency, albeit of a different sort. The rose outside Somlata's doorstep momentarily finds sustenance and space inside her bedroom, but she feels guilty after her husband returns from his travels and throws it out of the window. However, we are aware of her feelings of desire towards Rafique. Years later, when her daughter presents her with the poem-letters written by Rafique, the circle is complete. In an interview with journalist Maria Grazia Falà, Aparna Sen states, 'Somlata, for her part, functions very much within the patriarchal system, but negotiates a space for herself all the same by being gentle and understated, rather than aggressive.'

That Pishima was literate is demonstrated by her ability to assess the accounts of the shop and write down the names of a wide range of sarees which Somlata then sets about procuring for her shop. In fact, she informs us that she learnt maths while listening to the pundit who taught her brothers—a second-generation woman learner, which reminds one of Rassundari Devi's autobiography, *Amar Jiban*. Rassundari Devi was among the earliest women writers in Bengali literature.

Somlata is not only able to read and write, she also puts her considerable intelligence to work in order to eke out a handsome living. With Chaitali as a young college graduate, the narrative of women's liberation and emancipation is taken even further. A worldview that may involve a political standpoint as such was not at the disposal of either Rashmoni nor Somlata, but the political context of the Bangladesh Liberation War and Chaitali's involvement in it act as a link to complete the tropes of personal desire, economic independence and political will—all of which go into the making of a human being, especially a woman.

The Cigarette

In the penultimate scene of *Goynar Baksho*, Pishima's ghost (played by Moushumi Chatterjee) and her granddaughter Chaitali (played by Srabanti) are seen sitting on the terrace, enjoying a smoke—Chaitali with her cigarette and Pishima on her hookah—and the latter even asks the young girl to take a turn on the hookah, which Chaitali passes up with some reluctance. The two women sit there—the widow and the unmarried woman—talking about their shared dreams and memories. In fact, after the birth of Chaitali, people note her similarities with Rashmoni, and Pishima's ghost abandons Somlata. She has, it seems, found a new friend in Chaitali—a young spirit just like hers. She is bold and beautiful and is ready to take risks, and that is what perhaps endears her to Rashmoni. However, her freedom has come at a cost—Rashmoni's incarceration two generations ago and her own mother's sacrifice of the pleasures of a secret and passionate love affair. With this particular scene, the director invites the audience to reflect on how the restrictions imposed on women have changed over time, yet somehow women are not completely free. With Chaitali smoking and indulging in romantic relations before marriage, Sen grudgingly acknowledges that the position of women in society has evolved over a century; it also indicates that there is still a lot that women have to fight for. Chaitali must still hide her relationship from her family members and meet her lover in secret—the fact that her lover is the grandson of an erstwhile manservant of the family would surely not make things easier for her. However, one can hope that Chaitali, with her education, confidence, intelligence and selfless ways, will emerge triumphant in the face of odds.

This scene, in many ways, captures the essence of Aparna Sen's film. This is where the past meets the present, the old meets the new, and two visions of Bengal (usually a nostalgic one in most films)—before the Partition and during the Bangladesh War—find each other face to face.

Of her film, Aparna Sen said, 'A film can have many layers, and it can be appreciated from the narrative point of view, or you might try to get some message through the plot movement. But a director can never be preachy,

I have made the jewellery box, called *streedhan* (women's wealth), a metaphor centering which the lives, outlook and social positions of women spanning three different generations change.'

Goynar Baksho then emerges as a very personal tale of three women and a jewellery box spread over three decades, becoming a saga of lust, love and liberation. What the author as well as the filmmaker do is turn this usually stereotypical idea of women's fondness for jewellery into a powerful document of liberation and emancipation. The message gets all the louder and stronger because it is brought about through the agency of women. The box of jewels, which once symbolized the sexual and social repression of women in Pishima's world in the 1940s, is instrumental in turning a timid Somlata into a self-sufficient and confident working woman in the 1950s. Later still, it comes in handy during the Bangladesh Liberation War in the 1970s through a cheeky Chaitali.

The film comes full circle when it is revealed that the dilapidated house taken over by the Bangladeshi revolutionaries once belonged to Somlata's secret lover, the poet Rafique, where Chaitali finds his love poems written to her mother. In exchange for the baubles, Chaitali leaves behind for her mother the poems Rafique had written to her, which are no less valuable. Pishima's ghost sighs in pleasure and perhaps finally finds rest. The constant interplay of timelessness and changing times makes this film adaptation of Shirshendu Mukhopadhyay's novel a rare and enriching cinematic experience of recent times.

Beyond the Binaries

Mr. and Mrs. Iyer

Aparna Sen's *Mr. and Mrs. Iyer* was released in 2002, in the aftermath of the carnage in Godhra, Gujarat. The film is a restrained and compassionate account of ordinary individuals caught in the crosshairs of a communal riot that leaves devastation and misery in its wake. However, it was marketed as a love story set amidst communal riots.

Set in an unidentified place in the Himalayan foothills, it revolves around Meenakshi Iyer (played by Konkona Sen Sharma) who is travelling back to Calcutta with her baby son Santhanam. The first part of the journey is by bus, and among her fellow passengers is Raja Chowdhury (played by Rahul Bose), who has been requested by her parents to take care of her during the journey. In the meantime, a riot ensues, sparked off by the killing of a Muslim man and resulting in Muslims burning Hindu villages. A curfew prevents the movement of vehicles and people, and thus Raja and Meenakshi are thrown about together as they find it nearly impossible to continue their journey forward. She identifies him as her husband to save him despite her initial rejection of him as a Muslim man because of her conservative upbringing and caste prejudices. The bond of affection which springs up between the two seems to be Sen's message to the world at large: that this is the only way forward in a world divided by sectarian politics.

To express her strong views about communalism and the destruction it leaves in its wake, Sen uses the trope of the bus journey which becomes an experience that leaves none of its passengers unscathed. The film begins in a South Indian household where a baby and a mother are getting ready for a journey. Then the narrative moves to a bus stop where Meenakshi Iyer and her son are to board a bus to the plains to catch a train back to Calcutta. It is at this bus stop that she meets Raja Choudhary, the other principal character of Sen's story. Of the subject matter of *Mr. and Mrs. Iyer*, Sen said, 'I wanted to make a love story and I always wanted to make a film about a journey. I really do feel that an external journey is a very meaningful metaphor for an internal one because a journey opens you up to new experiences, you find out things about yourself and about others that you have hitherto not even expected.'

Communal violence has formed the subject matter of many a work in Indian cinema—from the violence unleashed during the Partition in 1947, right up to the Bombay riots in 1992, and finally the Godhra carnage and its aftermath. Since then, this violent episode in the history of modern India has found many a depiction on celluloid—*Firaaq* (2008) by Nandita Das and *Parzania* (2007) by Rahul Dholakia being two other films on the same issue. In an interview, Aparna Sen said that the backdrop of her story, however, was the 9/11 attacks.

Where Bollywood prefers an overdoing of emotions, Sen's film is rather understated and can even be called lyrical. It is about two strangers belonging to two different cultures and religions, who come together during the very brief period of a bus ride, spend two days together, and fall in love with one another. The backdrop to this—the killings—is mostly reported and none of it is allowed to spill over into *Mr. and Mrs. Iyer*'s love story. There are quieter and more contemplative moments in the story punctuated by killings and reports of violence coming in, but it is these moments which make the film special. Deepa Mehta's film *Earth* also reports on the violence which erupted during the Partition when India and Pakistan became two separate nation states; but while it comes across as a more gendered rendition of the same, Sen's approach is more humanitarian. Her film's protagonist Mrs Iyer gives up her caste prejudices to save the life of a man who has been nothing but kind and solicitous to her, but who nevertheless remains a stranger. It is only later that she finds out about his interests, worldview, habits, good qualities, and so on.

It is special because of another reason—the depiction of love between an upper-caste Hindu woman and a Muslim man, which is yet another delicate issue and usually not the staple fare of Indian cinema. *Mr. and Mrs. Iyer* can be labelled as middle cinema which tries to address the ethical issues that surface in the film. The focus is on individual conflicts rather than community issues, and the film is set in a vague area, although Sen said in an interview that it was set in the Himalayan foothills of North Bengal. One can say that in its own specific way, middle cinema can create a space for the recognition of fundamentalism or ethnic violence (issues which can possibly be resolved there)—a space created by the director that can reassess ethical issues and initiate a questioning of the unwritten moral code in contemporary Indian cinema.

The representation of women's agency has undergone vast changes in recent years, as has the treatment of communalism, yet there continues to be a sensitive area in which subaltern subjectivities—namely, Hindu women and Muslims—exist. *Mr. and Mrs. Iyer* is interesting because it refuses a neat closure or a clear-cut moral resolution. It appears to ask more questions than it answers, and in doing so, provides a platform for negotiation about how one should deal with extreme situations—in the narrative, Cohen, one of the passengers in the bus, in order to protect himself from the rioters, tells on an old Muslim couple who are then hauled off the bus and murdered.

The Partition remains a raw wound in the background of all films about India's multicultural make-up, with the representation of Muslims falling into two neat categories: one, as violent, bloodthirsty fanatics, and second, as sanitized, domesticated and patriotic middle-class liberals. Nevertheless, as in all Aparna Sen films, the Woman question becomes an overwhelming one—here, the upper-caste Hindu Brahmin woman overcomes her scruples and saves the life of one of her fellow Muslim passengers during an attack by Hindu rioters, while Raja, alongside the other men in the bus, fail to react as the elderly Muslim couple are being led away for slaughter. Only a young girl in the bus, who had hitherto mostly been seen to enjoy herself with her other friends, plucks up enough courage to protest.

In the course of the narrative, Raja and Meenakshi are forced to spend a night or two together in a wayside forest bungalow until they are able to catch a train back to the metropolis. This enforced intimacy compels them to engage with questions that involve each other's cultural milieu. Sen seems to be suggesting that her world is a closed but protected one. Her father usually travels with her to the city in the plains to put her on the train to Calcutta whenever she visits her parents in the hills. Even for this journey, her father requests Raja to take care of his daughter while Meenakshi appears slightly embarrassed about it. It seems that she has not been given space to think about things on her own, and her existence may even be a dull and humdrum one but she doesn't seem to mind it very much, even accepting it as it is. However, not until much later does she get to appreciate a different sort of lifestyle. While talking to Raja, she begins to understand lives lived differently from her own, hinting at some other kind of existence. Initially, Raja tries to draw Meenakshi into a debate that involves the irrationality of the caste system, but she refuses to enter the argument. Yet later, she changes herself.

Raja is a liberal who represents modern India while Meenakshi is someone who does not question traditional ideas of impurity and caste. Earlier, while they were engaged in play-acting as husband and wife, a gaggle of girls from the bus confronted them and demanded to know their love story. It was only when Raja started to weave the story that Meenakshi got to know him better. His stories about living in the middle of a forest in Wayanad, having dinner in a tree-house by the light of clay lamps, thrilled her beyond words.

However, Sen seems to be suggesting that despite having an MSc in physics, Meenakshi is still caught up in archaic, myopic customs and beliefs. However, Raja's conduct with her endears him to her and the two develop a friendship in which she begins to see him as another human being, rather than just a Muslim. She begins enjoying his company and even drinks water from his bottle, while earlier she felt defiled drinking from the same bottle. She begins enjoying little moments of intimacy—as much as a make-believe family of baby, mother and father can.

Through this episode, Sen seems to be suggesting a link between secular education and sociopolitical harmony forged through everyday interactions as the only way one can bring about some kind of enlightened tolerance. Meenakshi not only develops that, but also comes to know about the amount of unbridled courage she has by saving another person's life. Her conservative outlook is flung aside at the hint of danger that threatens the very lives of the passengers in the bus. Meenakshi decides then and there that she has seen enough meaningless violence in the name of religion to let the Hindu fanatics lead another innocent to the slaughter. She pushes Santhanam into Raja's lap so that he is rendered speechless, only to follow her lead to act as her make-believe husband in front of the rioters.

The Journey

The motif of the bus journey is symbolic of Meenakshi's inner journey as a person and she finds herself changed over its course. At the beginning of the journey, she is simply Mrs Iyer from a conservative and orthodox Tamil Brahmin family, who only partakes of vegetarian food and has set notions about the world at large. As the bus makes its way down to the plains below, she finds it more and more difficult to handle her young son on her own, who appears excitable and begins to cry. This irritates most of her other co-passengers until she turns to Raja for assistance; he helps her untiringly.

The scenes in the bus are revealing in the sense that they help delineate the passengers' characters. The bus consists of a motley crowd of predominantly Hindu Indians, except for a lone Jew and an elderly Muslim couple. The passengers represent a wide range of age, social, linguistic and religious differences. Among them are a group of young college students, a newly wedded couple, a middle-aged woman with a differently abled son, two Sikh men—one elderly, the other slightly younger, a group of Bengali men, and the protagonists, Meenakshi Iyer and Raja Choudhury.

The young college students seem carefree, given to singing and enjoying themselves, as is the wont of youth. At the back of the bus, the Bengali men play cards to while away their time. To the consternation of the woman with the disabled son, they also drink alcohol which the son, unable to understand, wishes to partake of.

In other words, the bus is a microcosm of India. The irritability expressed by many while adjusting to their co-passengers' presence and needs is an incredibly mimetic reflection of Indian society.

Having settled down, the passengers make their way down to the plains. However, in a short while, their bus gets stranded in the middle of a riverbed because of the riot that has ensued. By nightfall, they are surrounded by a band of Hindu fundamentalists. The extremists threaten to torch the bus if they do not cooperate and prove their Hindu credentials in a rather humiliating manner. Much like in other films, the Indian man is not portrayed in a flattering light and is shown to be ineffectual. When asked later about the reason for his action, Cohen blubbers that it was his neck which would have been on the line since a Jew is circumcised as well, and he could well have been mistaken for being a Muslim.

It is precisely at this moment that Meenakshi puts aside all her prejudices and lets her humanity take precedence over the scruples of religion, caste and creed. In this brief and defining moment of danger, her humanism comes to the fore. By portraying the utter irrationality and ineffectuality of the men in this situation, Sen seems to highlight the need to order one's priorities, and have the courage to defend common humanity over and above particularities that do not mean much.

By bestowing a new name on Raja—a sort of reversal of the wedding ceremony in which the man gives the wife a new name— Meenakshi grants him a new lease of life, calling him 'Mr Iyer'. In Sen's film, the woman becomes an agentic force and occupies the centre stage. She is not portrayed in absentia or as an object of male desire. The fact that she keeps her cool and confidently lies to the fanatics, and is also able to convince her co-passengers, enables her to confidently step out of a culturally defined space in defiance of patriarchal norms of behaviour.

One may well criticize the film for romanticizing a very complex problem and lumping together various forms of violence, but adding an individual and personal dimension to a problem possibly teaches us much more than mere theory. The film does not claim to have all the answers. Like Meenakshi Iyer, Aparna Sen could but only respond to the violence and madness unfolding around her on a personal level—as an artist. If one reads such situations carefully, one can see that at the heart of all violence is an individual out to destroy another individual.

Sati

Aparna Sen's *Sati* (1989) can be read from very many angles and that is perhaps why it is seminal to this book. For one, the obvious reading would be that of women's oppression. For some others still, it could be the portrayal of orthodox Hinduism and patriarchy. Whatever it may be, at the heart of the film is the oppression of Uma who is doubly marginalized for being a woman as well as a person with a disability. It is an era in which women are considered 'sati' when they can be burnt on the funeral pyres of their husbands, and it is a fact which is not only celebrated but also propagated. It is also an age in which the Brahmin reigns supreme and whatever he says goes; no one can question his views, not even another Brahmin.

Sen locates her story at a transitional time when the old is slowly giving way to the new. While the Kulin Brahmins add to women's oppression by marrying multiple women, Raja Ram Mohan Roy is also fighting for reforms within an orthodox Hindu society. Although none of that forms a part of the plot, Bachaspati, the oldest and most venerated Brahmin in the village, is heard referring to the social reformer derisively as 'that Dewan' when there is talk of the sati system being eradicated.

As is discernible then, there are several issues which are woven into the narrative of Sen's film. Uma, the protagonist of *Sati,* is of marriageable age, and lives with her aunt and uncle in a village in Bengal at the turn of the nineteenth century. She has speech and hearing disabilities which present her with unique challenges. She has a cousin who is also of marriageable age, but who cannot marry as Uma is older than her, and therefore must be wed earlier. Since she has a clause of widowhood in her horoscope, they decide to get her married to a tree. But in an age which glorified sati, marrying her off to a man would have surely fitted the bill. However, it is the fact that she has a speech and hearing disability which prevents her relatives from finding a husband for her. Uma is perhaps the most hardworking member of the family. While her uncle is the only person who seems positively inclined towards Uma, her aunt is less sympathetic to her condition. She seems to bear no love for her and wishes her dead. More than any other family member, Uma's aunt sees her as a burden and sides with her grandson Gopal whenever he and Uma fight.

Uma has no one in the world who can comfort her. Sen depicts her place of comfort as the hollow of a banyan tree near the riverside (to which she is later married). The tree, being unable to speak itself, can perhaps understand Uma and the suggestion here is that they can communicate, perhaps because they are kindred spirits. While Uma is doubly marginalized, other women are also oppressed. Ironically, it is women who add to the cycle of oppression. None of the women protest when Uma's older cousin goes off to marry a second time so that he can get some dowry to use it for his sister's marriage. When his wife gives birth to a daughter, there is disgust writ large on Uma's sister-in-law's face.

In this world, men are prized creatures and commodities. They extract money from their in-laws if they visit their house, and even charge money to spend the night with their wives. And all that the daughter of the family can do is pawn her gold bangle to raise the money, which obviously reveals her own physical desire and need for physical intimacy. This, again, is a recurring theme in Aparna's films—a raw exploration of female sexuality—a trope which is present right from the beginning of her filmmaking career, adding an interesting dimension to her films.

What makes the film *Sati* distinct is also the fact that it seeks to highlight the world of a disabled woman. This, again, is a recurring trope in Sen's films; *Paromitar Ek Din* and *15 Park Avenue* also deal with this issue to a great extent. They are all sensitive, sympathetic portrayals, even if the treatments may not always be realistic. For instance, Meethi's disappearance into thin air at the end of *15 Park Avenue* is just Sen taking recourse to magic realism, or it is her way of saying that there is no place for a person like Meethi in the so-called normal world, or again, that Meethi may have acquired agency and decided not to be a part of the 'normal' world.

While Uma may be the protagonist of *Sati*, the director seems to be highlighting the lack of choice experienced by all women. They are all, in a way, symbolically mute. When her uncle's son from another marriage turns up at the family home to talk about his mother's demise, Uma's uncle identifies him by his pet name 'Potol'. All that his wife can do is accept it as part of her fate and make room for the son from another marriage. But this oppression at the hands of patriarchy does not, in any way, give rise to female camaraderie. All that the women do is try to make the best of their situations, even at the cost of making the lives of other women miserable. None of the women characters in *Sati* are portrayed sympathetically. If anything at all, they side with the men and help in the perpetuation of heinous traditions.

On the night that Uma dies, felled by her tree husband in the terrible storm, she is refused shelter by her family members who have locked their doors and barred their windows to save themselves from the deluge. She is made to sleep in the cowshed, and soon enough, the straw roof is blown away and she is drenched along with the animals. While she leads them to the kitchen to save them from further harm, she herself seeks shelter from her tree husband. She believes that like all other times when it has provided shelter and comfort from certain unpleasant happenings, this time too, the tree would help tide her over. The fact that she is mute like the animals, in addition to being unwanted, makes her family members treat her the same way.

The schoolteacher Nabin, apparently a well-wisher of the family, is unable to exercise control over his wife who is the daughter of a rich man and who refuses to leave the comforts of Calcutta to come live with her husband in the village. So in effect, women are not totally powerless in this world. What determines their power is money. Since neither the hapless Uma nor her family members have any, Nabin, deprived of a conjugal life, takes sexual advantage of the helpless Uma since she cannot speak. So his secret is safe with her. However, the fact that she comes back to him yet again another night bespeaks her desire for sex, and Sen does not shy away from showing it. Ironically, it is this very act of Nabin's that leads to an awakening of desire in Uma. She seeks solace in the hollow of her tree husband but does not find it there, so she returns to Nabin. The idea of desire as an unknown, unexplored, unexpressed, unfulfilled and conflicting force returns again and again in each of her narratives. And in doing so, Sen does not restrict herself to female desire, although that is most acutely expressed and explored in many of her films. *Sati*, like many of her other films, is also deeply invested in exploring the relationships among human beings in society, and this is what makes her films different.

In this oppressive society, while women seem to be at the receiving end of subjugation, men are slightly better off since they can choose certain things. For instance, one of Uma's cousins chooses to remain unmarried, although his brother gets married twice. It is also the men who decide the women's fate while killing off a young girl by feeding her opium in the name of attaining sati-hood, or in the instance of asking Uma to get married to a tree. However, it is in her bond with her tree husband that Uma discovers her strength. Since she is ineligible to marry a human being owing to a faulty horoscope, she certainly takes her relationship with her tree husband more seriously.

It is not surprising given that the world of men cannot be depended upon. They do not act as protectors but are oppressors and are rather greedy. They also believe in rituals which cannot be questioned, not even by a Brahmin. The only person who does question Bachaspati's tenet to get Uma married to a tree is a young pupil training under him. No one else, not even Uma's uncle, dares question the diktat of the old Bachaspati who is obviously held in great esteem by the villagers, and perhaps also feared.

Uma's uncle seems ineffectual; he is not too advanced

in years, yet he feels the burden of responsibility too strongly. He mostly remains silent and keeps to himself, but remains perpetually worried about Uma. Yet he fails to protect her when the time comes. Even though he takes the first step in challenging Bachaspati's decision that Uma should get married to a tree, his will crumbles in the face of Bachaspati's overwhelming personality and he meekly submits to Uma's fate. Yet, immediately after he hands over his sister's meagre jewellery to Uma, having saved it for the occasion of her marriage, he dies—perhaps finally being free of his burden. His sons hardly seem to be doing anything; while the younger one keeps himself busy singing and playing musical instruments, the older one depends on whatever he can to get off his father-in-law. In fact, the lot of Kulin Brahmins seem to be getting on this way.

Sati is perhaps also about the oppression brought on by this particular caste. While the British rule and the efforts of Brahmo Samaj[14] reformers like Ishwar Chandra Vidyasagar, Raja Ram Mohan Roy, Dwarkanath Ganguly were aiming to better the lot of women at that time, it would be quite some time before it benefitted women like Uma or the young widow who was taken to the husband's pyre and burnt alive with great fanfare at the beginning of the film. They all participated in the heinous act and propagated the belief that being a sati was perhaps one of the greatest acts of a woman's life. It is because of such

[14]The Brahmo Samaj was a socio-religious reform movement founded by Raja Ram Mohan Roy in Bengal in 1828, advocating monotheism, rationalism and social reforms such as the abolition of sati and caste discrimination.

thinking that numerous women were subjected to such a horrible death in the name of religion.

Ironically, the highest rank in the caste hierarchy is assumed by men who are neither affluent nor powerful. They do not have a vocation to speak of either. Much like his sons, Uma's uncle Brahmapada Chatterjee, as iterated earlier, sits idle at home. When his son from another marriage appears, out comes a diary which he has been maintaining with details of his other wives.

There are several aspects to this problem and Aparna Sen does not rest by merely laying the blame or highlighting the victimization of Uma. Instead, she delves deep into the crisis at hand. Indeed, improving the lot of women is a constant and ongoing battle. Although their condition has become better since the nineteenth century—the time period that this film is set in—many things continue being the same.

Through her portrayals of women struggling within a patriarchal society, Sen perhaps wants to hit at the very heart of the problem. The oppressor himself or herself is oppressed. The Kulin Brahmins are burdened with the diktats of keeping their line pure as tradition would have it, along with keeping on running their households. As a character in the film puts it, running a family demands that he earn his keep from the several wives he marries. However, what is disheartening is that they do not seek to improve their lot by educating themselves and finding employment with the British rulers. Instead, they prefer the easier way out, namely, exploiting others—especially women. This reflects a lot on the inward-looking Brahmin community of the nineteenth century; in fact, Madhav Bachaspati's militant stand against the winds of change contributes to a great extent to what happens to Uma and the other women. He rouses the villagers by saying, 'These are bad times, Hinduism is facing a tremendous crisis. In Calcutta Vidyasagar with his new-fangled ideas is endangering our religion as well as our society. Widow remarriage! God have mercy on our souls, it is all the more important now that all Hindus rally together and save their sacred religion by rigidly following the scriptures.' One cannot say that much has changed—as far as the outlook on religion is concerned—in India. If at all, it has returned with a vengeance and secularism is on the wane.

However, one does not find the accusing finger being pointed at anyone in *Sati*. The film genuinely tries to focus on the humane and perhaps moral factors pertaining to sati. And once this has been attempted, several other threads begin unravelling. For instance, the film also explores the victimization of poor high-caste Brahmins. They are also commodities in the marriage market—not any less than women. Being a medium that operates on a strict timeframe, a film cannot go on to explore the complexities of the social system at large, examining the nitty-gritty of the hierarchy operating within the community of Brahmins as well. However, a discerning audience member or critic won't fail to make the connection. One still gets a sense of the way they try to keep body and soul together in the wake of oppression.

Lest one gets carried away by pity, Sen ensures that she demonstrates how these very victims then go on to victimize their destitute relatives who are forced to depend on their goodwill for their very survival, Uma being a case in point. When Brahmapada expresses his unwillingness to marry Uma to a tree because it is difficult to get a suitable groom for her, Girijaya, his wife, expresses her rancour and displeasure. The first thing that crosses her mind is the thought of dowry: 'And after marriage every year her husband will come to collect money from us! Do you think any family will take a girl like that home? And if they do, we will lose a valuable working hand. There is always so much to do around here. I am getting old. Shashibala will be married soon and will go to her in-laws. How will Sabitri manage alone with two small children and another one on the way? This is the best arrangement. A peepul tree is not hard to find. There is one by the riverside where she spends all her time.'

The logic of victimization then, one can safely surmise, rests largely on the nexus of labour and money. Uma is nothing but a free working hand, looking after several things in the household. It also rests on the fact that the victim can turn into an oppressor when the opportunity arises. The women do not sympathize with each other, and this is borne out through several incidents in the narrative of the film itself. When a calf is born to their cow immediately after the daughter-in-law of the family Sabitri delivers a girl child, Shashibala actually expresses joy that it is a she-calf while being dismissive of her newborn niece.

Sabitri can only accept the pain and humiliation in silence. Even as her husband embarks on a second marriage, and it means a depreciation of her role and importance in the household, she remains but a mute spectator to it all. The only person who finally does protest her lowly status in the family is Uma, who screams and hits her aunt in the second half of the film. Indeed, she comes to acquire some sort of agency after her marriage.

While one could well call her treatment at the hands of Nabin sexual exploitation, the fact that she returns to him is an interesting aspect added to the already layered film. This shows that Aparna Sen is keen on being mimetic and that reality constantly impinges on her fictional world. It is never a black-and-white one, just as real life too is inexplicable. It also adds a human dimension to Uma who, for the most part, remains a mystery to her family members. While her aunt and uncle discuss the pros and cons of getting married to a peepul tree, she remains oblivious to the discussion while carrying on with her daily chores. Although she is not able to express herself through words, her large expressive eyes convey wonder, desire, fear and loathing.

Although, as shown in the film, women in society are powerless, it does not end there. They are also at the centre of this power struggle. The film begins and ends with the deaths of various women, traditions being the common factor in both cases. It is the body of the woman which becomes the site on which tradition is debated and later reformed. But at no point in the narrative does it come down to being a clichéd and hackneyed representation of women. However, Sen's film does invite comparison, and one finds intertextual echoes from other times and other spaces in Indian cinema.

One is especially reminded of Ray's film *Devi* (1960) in this regard. Doyamoyee, the central figure in Ray's narrative, offers to his audience much greater complexity—is she a victim, or is the malaise far more deep-rooted? Ray, however, makes it difficult for his audience to reach any particular conclusion, and for the most part, leaves it ambiguous.

Curiously enough, Sen's *Sati* reminded me of Satyajit Ray's *Pather Panchali* as well, especially the figure of Durga in it. And if one does indeed go back to its source—the novel from which it was adapted onscreen—one finds the pathos-ridden figure of Indir Thakrun, yet another victim of the Kulin *pratha*. Writer Bibhutibhushan Bandyopadhyay indeed went on to explicate about Indir Thakrun's life in some detail, thus humanizing her a great deal instead of reducing her to a mere case study. Indir, who cannot remember her husband for the simple reason that he never visited her since the wedding night, however, was blessed with a daughter from the union. The daughter nevertheless died in childhood, and so Indir came to invest her love in young Durga, who also reciprocated her aunt's love. Indeed, one can say the same about Sen's handling of this problem. In spite of being a victim of society, especially its traditions, Uma is invested with a certain kind of dignity; quiet even in death, she finally attains the much-acclaimed status of satihood. As Madhav Bachaspati and his train of priests, along with the other men of the village, look with wonderment at the scene of devastation: Uma's prone body guarded by inanimate hands—the branches of her tree husband—protectively encasing her within its folds even as it fell.

Even though Uma cannot enunciate it verbally, Sen chooses to delineate her problem by situating it in a milieu that needs excavation on film. Without reducing it to didacticism of any sort, Sen effectively portrays and examines the sociocultural context of the film that forces her audience to sit up. Sen's *Sati* also invites comparison to Girish Kasaravalli's film *Ghatashraddha* (1977), which deals with women's oppression at the hands of the powers that be. In this film, although Yamuna is not disabled, she is also reduced to being a mute spectator as patriarchy, in the guise of Brahmins, flexes its muscles.

While in *Sati* Madhav Bachaspati does get questioned by his young pupil, Kasaravalli inserts into his narrative a young Brahmin boy who acts as a witness to Yamuna's trials and tribulations. While Sen's film ends on a note of finality—a note of divine justice in particular, Kasaravalli chooses to have an open ending in his film as the young boy leaves Yamuna's father's school because Yamuna brought shame to it by having an illicit relationship and getting impregnated. However, one cannot be too sure that the young boy will not grow up to become an oppressor as well. After all, he too belongs to the same sect of Brahmins that deem Yamuna's ostracization and banishment from the village as just punishment.

However, when Uma gets impregnated by Nabin and her condition is discovered, the womenfolk of the family do not publicize it. They quickly manage to solve the problem by seeking a natural way of terminating Uma's pregnancy; they also do nothing to seek the culprit. They treat her in a less than sympathetic manner, isolating and ostracizing her, which finally results in her death. While Sen's *36 Chowringhee Lane* and *Parama* both advocate women's agency while they come to something of an understanding about themselves, *Sati* comes to highlight a time when 'choice' was a forbidden word for both the sexes. While women became obvious victims of tragic circumstances brought on by tradition and patriarchy, men also found themselves to be victims of another sort.

Becoming and the Question of the Self

At the end of Aparna Sen's *Parama* (1985), the eponymous heroine says, 'But I don't have any guilt feelings,' and completely switches herself off, having at last discovered her own identity and sense of self. This discovery is to the dismay and horror of all, especially the doctor and the husband—a situation that is all too transparent. One wonders whether this ought to be the status quo for all Indian women, especially the dissenting ones and the silent sufferers.

Parama happens to be Sen's second film after she created a revolution in the cine-world with her debut film *36 Chowringhee Lane* (1981). She appeared on the scene when alternate cinema was slowly dying a painful death due to the onslaught of masala movies that were being churned out by Bollywood, which, by the way, are still celebrated and much feted.

Aparna Sen also made her debut at a time when non-mainstream women directors were almost unheard of in India—except for Sai Paranjpye and Kalpana Lajmi who made their debuts in 1974 and 1986 respectively. *Parama* was a film helmed by a woman director who sought to adorn her cinema with women's aesthetics and produce an example of a counter-cinema. The director in Sen fought a bitter fight to make a place for herself in the male-dominated pantheon of directors. And what a fight it must have been to present the story of a 40-something housewife (Parama) who indulges in an extramarital affair with her nephew's photographer friend called Rahul, loses her family in the process, and regains her sense of self and identity! This Aparna Sen achieved through subversion, bringing to the fore Parama's hidden alienation, her socialization and ultimate redemption. For what else is Rahul but a means to awaken and identify the 'woman' in her?

Invisible Oppression and the Woman Question in *Parama*

Parama opens with a series of photographic frames capturing the various nuances of the Durga Puja, with the protagonist Parama at the centre. The various frames depict the eponymous heroine feeding the deity *sandesh* (as per the puja norms), looking back as one of her numerous relatives calls out to her for help in performing the *sindoor khela.* In all these frames, even though the traditional Bengali (Indian) woman is captured, the essence of Parama is missing. 'Parama' is another name for Durga, the almighty goddess in the Hindu pantheon. In the film, the heroine Parama is playing a subservient role—that of an aunt, wife, housewife and mother. We miss the 'power' that is inherent in the name 'Parama'. Aparna Sen, who chooses to name her heroine Parama—which is almost always used as a prefix meaning the ultimate woman or the incomparable one—uses it as a satire of the restrictive nature of women's identities in a patriarchal society. The paradox lies in the incomparability between the two as Parama, Aparna Sen's heroine, subsumes her own identity in the many relationships she has with other people while having none to call her own. Even though exquisitely beautiful and almost a perfect mother, aunt, wife, and daughter-in-law, she is ultimately reduced to a 'nothing'.

Parama, the protagonist, is quite happy with this effacement and the viewer fails to notice her own alienation from her real self. She is more than happy, willing and content to play the various roles—*ma* (mother), *kakima* (younger paternal uncle's wife), *boudi* (elder brother's wife; sister-in-law), *chhoto bouma* (younger son's wife)—that confuse Sara, Rahul's American assistant. Sara is forced to ask Parama: 'What is your real name?' It is a genuine enquiry and one that could be asked of many Indian women who have conflated socialization with acculturation to such an extent that they have effaced their own identity in the process. Even on being asked such a pertinent question, Parama does not answer. It is her husband who does; 'It is Parama,' he says simply and smiles. Parama's nephew Bubu adds 'Chowdhury', her husband's family name, which acts as a traditional marker for all married Indian women. Her worth in the Chowdhury family is determined by her ability to perform her roles suitably. Parama's life sheds light on the socialization of all women in Indian society, where a woman is circumscribed by an invisible *Lakshmanrekha* (a marker of the limit of her independence, a sure cause for alienation). A woman's socialization[15] takes place in a way that inevitably subjugates her to an extremely narrowly defined lifestyle.

This socialization has taught her how to behave exactly like 'a woman', and conditioned her into becoming the ideal subject: the ideal wife, the ideal mother. A man is never subjected to such socialization. Indian society, in fact, initially celebrates his birth and then proceeds to hand over all sorts of privileges to him. These separate socializations of the girl child and the boy child exist across all strata of Indian society. It is, in fact, even stricter in the upper classes which, while giving off the impression of having liberal attitudes, tend to be far more hypocritical and stricter in terms of controlling the bodies of their women. The woman is taught to subsume her own identity in the face of other roles which she must perform. Right from childhood, a woman, especially in the Indian context, is taught that her father's house is never her own, and she is almost always described in terms of being the wealth—honour and chastity—of the family. Thus circumscribed in mind and body, she leaves her natal home for that of

[15]Gender socialization in India starts from the moment children are born, where the birth of a female child is not usually welcome. In certain states such as Haryana, Punjab and Rajasthan, female foeticide is still practised. An interesting read on this is Mary E. John's 'Sex ratios and sex selection in India: History and the present', in the *Routledge Handbook of Gender Studies,* edited by Leela Fernandez, pp. 291–304, Routledge, New York, 2018. From an early age, girls are told that they will be leaving their natal home once they are married, and they are called *paraya dhan* (someone else's wealth), whereas the birth of a male child is welcomed. Male children's education is much focused on because it is believed that they will not only add to the family wealth but also look after the parents when they are old.

her husband (which, again, is not her own; it belongs to her father-in-law). She is taught, from birth till death, that a woman is never her own person; she belongs to the various men in her life—in the beginning her father, then her husband, and finally her son.

I now turn back to the film that is at the heart of this chapter. The state of 'learned helplessness' of the Indian woman is highlighted by the director through telling shots, and especially through the camera of Rahul Roy, Bubu's New York-based photographer friend. Parama is first espied working for the Durga Puja. The Durga festival is celebrated by Bengalis with much fanfare for five days. They worship the Goddess Durga who is blessed by the pantheon of male gods. They bless her with divine *shakti* and a plethora of weapons for each of her 10 hands. She goes on to kill the demon king Mahishashura, and saves heaven from being overrun by him and his cohorts. It appears that Parama, much like Durga, sprouts 10 hands while tending to the various puja rituals as well as the needs of her relatives and family members. But despite the strength of the goddess whom she worships, who has an identity of her own, Parama lacks her own identity. There is thus a huge gap between self, identity and active role performance. Parama is the perfect and typical wife, daughter-in-law and mother, and nothing beyond that.

It is Rahul who takes the initiative to get to know the real 'Parama', and is indeed the first person to address her by her name while all the other actors in her life insist on calling her by some socially defined name based on her relationships with other people. In fact, her husband refers to her as 'shunchho' or 'ogo', which roughly translates to 'hey, are you listening?', reducing the person being addressed to a non-player.

Christine Delphy and Diana Leonard, in their rather fascinating article 'The Variety of Work Done by Wives', make the point that wives contribute to their husbands' welfare not only in terms of looking after their comforts at home, but also in enhancing their ability to earn a livelihood. Wives provide moral support and also contribute to unpaid domestic labour. Similarly, Sallie Westwood's article 'Domestic Labourers or Stand by your Man—While He Sits Down and Has a Cup of Tea', provides ideas about how the oppression of women takes places within social and familial life where the roles of wives and mothers are highlighted even in places of work. I read this as nothing more than an attempt to keep women in check. I find this analysis useful as a worldview that keeps Parama in check.

Almost as a counterfoil to this character is Sheela, Parama's friend, who, having set up a school for children with cerebral palsy, divorces her husband willingly when he chooses to leave for better opportunities in Bombay. As Parama talks about this with her daughter and her mother-in-law, her young daughter Esha states that it is indeed commendable that Sheela has been able to move out of her husband's life and establish a life of her own while her own mother lives a secondary life in the shadow of her father. Although Esha provides one of the first dissenting voices in Aparna Sen's film, it is bookish knowledge that she expresses. Later in the narrative when her mother Parama flouts societal norms by having a lover, Esha appears almost distant and judgemental.

The Politics of Shame

The protagonist Parama's agonized self-reflection is, to a certain extent, based on her own ideas about respectability. Parama's aunt Sudha Pishi's incarceration in a room within the family home, and the socialization and acculturation brought about by society via her natal family members, leave her with a deep sense of anxiety and fear. Tamara Sheffer and Sally Munt argue: 'Shame and shaming are also bound up with social inequality, both reflecting and serving to reinforce, reinstate and legitimise social injustice. Shame is closely entangled with gender subjectification and normative gender binarisms, which are raced, classed and enmeshed with other forms of intersectionalities.'[16]

To a large extent, Parama's ostracization is brought about by notions of what an ideal woman should be like. Society restricts a married woman to the roles of the ideal wife and/or mother. Her husband and other men do not have any such demands made upon them by society. In fact, the subjugation of women gives the men free rein to pursue whatever they want—be it in terms of professional choices, personal ambitions or their unbridled sexuality. So while Bhaskar Choudhury is free to make a pass at his secretary in a hotel room in Bombay, Parama is forbidden to go out of doors. Even her limits as well as her desires are circumscribed by others.

This division of male and female socialization is well depicted in the film, indicating a deeply ingrained gender

---

[16]Sheffer, Tamara, and Sally Munt, 'A feminist politics of shame: Shame and its contested possibilities', *Feminism & Psychology*, Vol. 29, No. 2, 2019, pp. 145–56.

politics that results in differential power positions. The woman's shame and guilt are not her own creations, but have been imposed on her via social norms, beliefs and customs. Sheffer and Munt's argument becomes particularly relevant when they say, 'Shame is imbricated within intersectional gender inequalities, with shame serving as a mechanism of surveillance and policing of gender binarisms in maintaining idealised, "respectable" femininity.'[17]

When her affair with Rahul is discovered, thanks to a very callous gesture on Rahul's part (or is it an intentional statement of defiance by the director against patriarchy?) whereby he sends across the *Life* magazine with Parama's semi-nude photo and a handwritten note saying 'Remember?', her husband finds it very difficult to accept it. Very soon, the whole family comes to know about Parama's transgression and various family members begin to comment on her behaviour.

Parama takes to her bed shunning all family members and living in a darkened claustrophobic room which even her children are not allowed to visit. Perhaps they choose not to of their own volition. And when the youngest relents, Parama bursts into tears. It is perhaps an internalized response to sociocultural gendered ideals and her failure to live up to them that trigger her maternal shame. The family then goes about silencing and othering her in a well-planned manner. The husband first goes about alienating her by asking the elderly woman who works as a maid in

[17]Sheffer, Tamara, and Sally Munt, 'Domestic labourers: Or stand by your man—while he has his cup of tea', *Gender: A Sociological Reader*, Jackson Stevi and Scott Sue (eds.), Routledge, London and New York, 2002, p. 146.

the household to look for his cufflinks. This is a deliberate attempt to insult Parama because she was the one who always looked after his needs. When she protests, he asks the maid to help him remove his personal belongings to the guest room. When Parama tries to stop this from happening and questions his actions, he maintains a deliberate silence. It is she who raises the question whether he is, in fact, not feeling a sense of loathing for her.

The 'othering' of Parama continues in other ways as well. Her mother-in-law, whom she has served so faithfully for many years, turns her face away from Parama and asks her to leave. Everyone else acts in an awkward manner around her, while her older son seems quite angry and disgusted (a typical male response). In such cases, it becomes clear that shaming occurs in a systematic and ruthless manner only for women. Had Bhaskar, her husband, indulged in an affair, it would have been considered normal and Parama would have been expected to accept the 'truth'. A hegemonic vigilance over perceived sexual transgressions is applicable only in the case of women, and in this case, Parama.

The Politics of Identity

Like Rahul who is a freelance photographer, Parama could well have been a successful professional having considerable skills, had she not been constrained and socialized in a particular way. When she goes out with Rahul for the first time, she is re-introduced to her own city from the top of an unfinished flyover, which makes her see it in a whole new light. At the same time, Rahul also gets introduced to a totally new Parama who beautifully recites poetry for him. At the same time, she announces that whatever she liked does not matter any longer in the life which she now leads. She reveals more about herself, which makes Rahul look at her anew. After meeting Rahul, she thinks of taking up a job and approaches Sheela, her friend, for help. However, since Parama did not graduate because she was 'married off', she is prevented from applying for jobs.

The director emphasises that Parama's affair with Rahul helps her find her true self. It prompts her to recall her childhood self, her sitar lessons with her teacher on the balcony, and the incarceration of her Sudha Pishi which she suddenly recalls on climbing up to the rooftop. She returns to playing the sitar as an expression of the fulfilment which she finds not only in being with Rahul (which she obviously does not find with her husband), but also in discovering older joys and pleasures along with a sense of self.

What is perhaps important here is what Kwame Anthony Appiah denounces as a problem of the term 'identity', which tries to subsume everyone within the same identity. He states that there are heterogeneous groups even within a seemingly similar group, displaying what he calls 'idem'—sameness.[18] However, the politics of identity here is played out quite differently—the many different roles are used to gag Parama into submission; her roles as a mother, wife, sister-in-law, daughter-in-law and aunt (which her family prefers and holds in high esteem) subsume her identity as a woman, and more importantly, as a human being with desires and a mind of her own.

---

[18]Appiah, Kwame Anthony, 'The politics of identity', *Daedalus,* Vol. 135, No. 4, 2006, pp. 15–22.

When her family rejects her, Parama attempts suicide by cutting herself in the bathroom. A timely warning from the old maid of the family saves her and gives her a new life. Even as she is recovering, the family tries to 'manage' her, especially her husband who, along with the doctor, advises her to be counselled by a psychiatrist, thus questioning her thinking capabilities. However, now the new Parama refuses to be managed and questions the veracity of such treatment, confusing the doctor and her husband with her questions. She also expresses a desire to forge an identity for herself by working as a salesperson selling sarees at the Kendriya Bhandar. This idea appals her husband and he questions her decision, 'Why do you want to work? Is my salary not enough? Bhaskar Chowdhury's wife work? I will increase your pocket money if you so wish.' To which she gives a resounding reply, 'But even that would be your money.' While this idea leaves her husband dumbfounded, Parama's daughter Esha looks at her mother with renewed respect. This is the mother whom she earlier failed to understand and support.

This backlash, as Laurie Rudman and Peter Glick state in their article 'Prescriptive Gender Stereotypes and Backlash Toward Agentic Women', stems from the fact that men's dependence on women (for sex, sexual reproduction, homemaking and child care) creates incentives for them to ensure that women remain deferent, compliant and willing to enact subordinate roles. As a result of women's increasing mobility towards the paid workforce, they have started to view themselves, and to be viewed by others, as being more agentic.[19] Although these changes might threaten the status quo, this potential challenge is undermined by continuing prescriptions for female communality (the traits of submission), such as encouraging women to imbibe certain traits of behaviour and value family life, marriage and children more than their professional lives. These prescriptions continue to this day in India, even though women have proved their worth professionally in various fields.[20]

One can perhaps read the treatment of Parama after her 'indiscretion' has been exposed and her suicide attempt as a means of punishing the transgressing woman who is supposed to live a life that her in-laws and husband, his family and society impose on her or circumscribe for her. This Lakshmanrekha, if crossed, can have dire consequences for the woman as is evinced by the film. While it is perfectly normal for a man to transgress, society and the woman's family are especially unforgiving in case it is a woman, and there is inevitably a backlash.

Aparna Sen ends the film with hope in the form of Esha accepting her mother's new identity by aligning with her thinking and her love for a special plant. Even Parama lets the image of Rahul be blown away with the wind—a symbolic representation of her own freedom from the past and her newfound courage to be her own self.

---

[19]Rudman, Laurie, and Peter Glick, 'Prescriptive gender stereotype and backlash toward agentic women', *Journal of Social Issues,* Vol. 57, No. 4, 2001, pp. 743–62, https://tinyurl.com/mrmafkt2. Accessed on 28 February 2025.

[20]Rudman and Glick, 'Prescriptive gender stereotype'.

Paromitar Ek Din

Paromitar Ek Din (2000) is an interesting film because of the portrayal of a pluralistic feminism in which Aparna Sen shows women being able to enact their choices more maturely. It also depicts women bonding in a way which is quite rare in films, because in this case, it is the bond between a mother-in-law and her daughter-in-law—usually seen as antagonists in society. Through the film, Sen also studies the position of the disabled woman in Indian society.

The film begins in the present day with Paromita attending her mother-in-law's funeral ceremony. Some of the events on this particular day help trigger her memories back to 14 years ago, when she first entered the household as daughter-in-law to the family. The film moves back and forth in time to include all of Paromita's key memories that highlight the main relationships in her life. Sen's deft plotting of *Paromitar Ek Din* through the trope of memories makes it a rather remarkable film within her oeuvre. It is also unusual in the sense that no filmmaker has attempted to work on such a subject before.

The trope of female camaraderie has always included friendship between friends of the same age, or mothers and daughters beginning as antagonists and later turning into friends. Rituparno Ghosh, for instance, portrayed the frayed relationship of a mother-daughter duo in *Unishe April* which ultimately got resolved through a crisis. The point of view in the narrative emerging in Aparna Sen's film is solely that of Paromita, as certain events on the day of the *shraddha* ceremony triggers certain memories of hers.

Whereas a differently abled man is considered unfortunate and an object of pity, a woman in the same position becomes a cause of shame and humiliation for the family. Khuku in *Paromitar Ek Din,* along with Uma (*Sati*) and Meethi (*15 Park Avenue*), are specially abled women who are marginalized due to their deviation from the socially and politically constructed norm of able-bodied men and women. In fact, along with these earlier films, the disabled 'other' is also studied in great depth here. Sen endows her special women with alternative ways of being. She rejects the superficial medical and cultural standards for cognitive and physical ability, and by portraying their inner worlds with great sensitivity, attempts to resist their marginalization, silencing or absence.

This retelling of Paromita's memories is somewhat linear; for instance, it begins in the beginning but does not include very detailed descriptions of her activities in the Sanyal household. Her husband Biresh is an uncouth, loutish kind of person in contrast to her sophisticated, mature behaviour. She is from south Calcutta which is a different world compared to the older, northern parts of the city, and this comes across in Biresh's inflections of speech, with the hard 's' sound—a dialect typical of the north. But Paromita sets these differences aside and embraces her new family. In this anamnesis, the differences between Sanaka, her mother-in-law, and Pramathesh, her father-in-law, also come to light, as does the position of the women in the household. The sons pay obeisance to the father because he is the earning member of the family. He also comes across as boorish and domineering, making demands on his wife and treating the women as scum. He is hardly seen to engage with his daughter Khuku at all, who is always living in her own world. In this family, the worlds of the women and the men seem to be separate, and money becomes an important factor.

Sanaka loves watching television serials but she also caters to the various demands of the family—cooking, looking after her differently abled daughter and sundry other matters. But her own desires and wants are never allowed to be enacted. One such incident which Paromita recalls is how her father-in-law Pramathesh, in a sadistic move, made Paromita switch off the television so that Sanaka could attend to him. The gender roles in the Sanyal household are clearly demarcated. The women, especially Sanaka and Paromita, are clearly neglected by their husbands as far as their desires and wants are concerned; they are expected to perform the role of dutiful wives catering to the physical demands of their husbands and are usually left to fend for themselves. Biresh shows a deep concern and affection for Khuku, which only amounts to getting upset if people talk about her sanity, whether it is his newly wedded wife or even his mother. He is never seen to look after Khuku in any other way. His own son Bablu, afflicted with cerebral palsy, however, remains neglected and perhaps even detested by him.

When Paromita's son Bablu is declared a 'spastic', Paromita's father-in-law immediately blames his daughter-in-law for the tragedy. They are an old-fashioned family who constantly reiterate the fact that a son is far more valuable than a daughter. The women shackled to the interiors remain neglected and are seen as people whose only duties are producing children or catering to the needs of their husbands.

Confined to domesticity, Sanaka is deprived of a great

many pleasures. There are sudden emotional outbursts when she bemoans her captive state. During these times, Khuku seems like a burden to her too, but Sanaka is also the only one who looks after her. However, she often forgets to give Khuku her medicines, which control her behaviour but can never cure her. Khuku is possibly one of the most marginalized members of this family, perhaps even doubly marginalized—first as a woman and second, as a patient of schizophrenia. It is an interesting depiction because Indian cinema hitherto almost always avoided representing the differently abled onscreen. Therefore, Sen's efforts become important, although the depiction itself may not be perfect. In the film, Khuku is a wonderful singer of Rabindrasangeet; blessed with a rich voice, singing is something that comes naturally to her. Perhaps Sen wanted to stress the fact that her family, who equate any mental illness with madness, failed to give Khuku either the medical treatment or her due through their negligence.

While Sanaka later finds a friend in Paromita, Khuku remains the loneliest. Her moments of loneliness are whiled away by taking up the *tanpura* and giving vent to her feelings by singing Tagore's songs. When she sings, she becomes oblivious to the world around her, having completely immersed herself in the act of singing, leaving onlookers and listeners mesmerized. She also experiences moments of clarity and asks some rather shrewd questions; for instance, as TV reports about various incidents of violence in the world come in, she asks whether the people who commit the acts of violence have the same kind of mental illness as she does. Political statements of such kinds, overt or otherwise, often feature in Sen's films. And in several of her interviews, she has often been quoted as claiming to be a humanist rather than a feminist. Sen seems to say that Khuku's one great deprivation is the fact that even though she has a deep desire to marry and be a mother, she will forever remain deprived of its joys and sorrows.

While there is an attempt by Sen to depict in a realist manner the workings of a conservative Bengali household of north Calcutta, the portrayal of Khuku's schizophrenia wherein it is reduced to madness sticks out like a sore thumb. Even in *15 Park Avenue,* Meethi's schizophrenia is less sympathetically judged by highly educated people who make no effort to understand her. There is also an underlying suggestion that this mental illness is inextricably tied up with sexuality and the desire for sex.

Khuku also seems to act like a channel for Sanaka to give vent to her feelings, and she takes it out on the poor woman whenever she feels frustrated at her lot. She beats up Khuku on several occasions instead of treating her with kindness and understanding. It is only later when the unschooled Sanaka begins taking Bablu to a 'spastic centre' does she begin to appreciate their inner worlds. Her family members deem it a curse inflicted by God when differently abled children are born in their household. The men, instead of taking care of them, find it easier to lay the blame on the woman or the mother for giving birth to such children.

Much like his father, Paromita's husband Biresh appears to be insensitive to his wife's needs or desires. He is not her idea of a good husband either and does not grow to be a confidante or friend to her. Even on the day of his wedding, he comes back late while Paromita falls asleep, tired of waiting for him. He also flares up when the new bride asks him about Khuku's illness. He equates schizophrenia with madness without even going into the intricacies of the disease himself. To the family members, Khuku's presence is a matter of shame. Although he appears to be fond of her, he does not bother to take care of her, relegating it instead to his wife and his mother while he pursues the more manly occupation of earning a living and going around with a girlfriend.

When a son is born to Paromita and Biresh, his parents proudly announce him as the heir to the Sanyal household, while Biresh looks on proudly for having fathered a son. However, a couple of months later when the child is diagnosed with cerebral palsy, Biresh does not hesitate to pronounce him dead. Afterwards, most of the sequences in the narrative that are centred on Bablu portray the women of the family as fussing around him and taking care of him. To the men, 'abnormal' children such as Khuku and Bablu are not to be presented to outsiders and are meant to be hidden away.

It is only much later when Bablu is about five that Paromita takes him to a spastic centre where both Sanaka and she discover their unique world through interacting with them. It is also here that Paromita meets her second husband Rajeev Srivastava, a documentary filmmaker who is making a documentary on the centre's work.

The interaction between the two leads to friendship and they decide to marry, but not without Sanaka resenting it. Rajeev appears to be more caring than Biresh as he solicitously asks her about her background and announces his intention to get her a job at an advertising firm. Paromita, whose afternoons were spent taking care of Bablu and his needs, now finds herself free to take up a job that suits her level of education. She was a student of comparative literature at Jadavpur University and later studied mass communication, but being part of a conservative family, was unable to work until then.

In the meantime, Biresh manages to acquire a girlfriend for himself since his relationship with Paromita is almost over. He, like his father, pays a lot of attention to his physical desires and since his wife refuses to have any relations with him, he decides to fend for himself. Later, after divorcing Paromita, he marries the same woman.

After her marriage to Rajeev, Paromita apparently seems to be happy and fulfilled. Her barren, unhappy marriage of 14 years comes to an end with Bablu's death. Bablu's presence brought Sanaka and Paromita closer together over the years, and they forged a bond that was perhaps even stronger than the one shared by Sanaka and Khuku.

The two seem to have been thrown together because of the tragedy of bearing differently abled children. Sanaka sympathizes with Paromita because she realizes that she is less than happy with Biresh, but as is the lot of women, has to bear the burden of it throughout her life. Sanaka confides in Paromita that she was ready to elope with Manimoy—who still visits her after all these years—leaving her children and husband behind, unafraid of how society would judge her. For a woman with such thoughts of revolt in her head, she presents a contradictory picture when it comes to treating her own daughter with love and affection instead of seeing her mental illness as a curse.

Despite feeling oppressed by her family, especially her husband, Sanaka finds it within herself to still see Manimoy—whom she had once loved and wished to marry—on a regular basis. She even helps him financially with money of her own. It is not Pramathesh's money, she points out chidingly to Manimoy; it is part of a life insurance policy that her brother had taken out in her name. Sanaka's limited economic emancipation is invaluable to her. This is also another trope that is close to Aparna Sen's heart and is treated in a big way in her later film *Goynar Baksho*.[21] Pramathesh and his sons find it irksome that he comes to see Sanaka but can do nothing about it. Like the other men in the narrative, Manimoy's portrayal is not flattering either, and he comes across more as a failure and a coward.

Interestingly, Manimoy (played by Soumitra Chatterjee) had once played the titular role in Satyajit Ray's *Kapurush* (1965). Could this be a nod to Ray's film in some way? Sanaka even tells Paromita that men fail at relationships, and nothing better is to be expected of them either. While Manimoy continues to play Sanaka's erstwhile love interest, feeble and dependent on Sanaka, Pramathesh is soon dispatched from the narrative via an accident which is merely reported. Such a treatment strengthens the suspicion that he was never important to Sanaka, nor to the script. The two sons appear dispensable as well—perhaps reflecting Sen's views about men in general.

Instead, female camaraderie comes to be highlighted to a greater extent. Sanaka suddenly blossoms after Pramathesh's death. Contrary to beliefs prevalent in Indian society—specially where the husband is worshipped as god and seen as a woman's universe, and whose absence means unhappiness and spells doom for the woman or the widow—Sanaka seems to savour the freedom. She is finally able to watch her Bengali serials in peace and whenever

[21]Personal interview with me.

she wishes to, without anyone ever chiding her. She even takes to flying kites on the rooftop with her grandchildren and her prodigious kite-flying skills leave Paromita amazed.

Marriage seems to have robbed her of many pursuits which once gave her immense pleasure. She tells Paromita that she had once been an expert swimmer and competed with her brothers, and that she could recite poems from memory; she even surprises Manimoy, who then quotes Sanaka's poem verbatim to Paromita and praises it. He then proceeds to tell Paromita about a young Sanaka who was once lively and had a prodigious memory. Khuku's illness seems to have sapped all her energy; this is Manimoy's guess about the changed Sanaka who appears to snap at every little thing.

However, even though Manimoy and Sanaka are emotionally close, it is Paromita's second marriage and consequent departure from the household that breaks her heart and makes her lonely once again. She falls gravely ill and dies soon after. It is with Paromita that she shares the greatest bond—something that even blood relatives don't share. Sanaka opens her heart to Paromita, and the two women find solace and love in each other which are otherwise missing from their lives. Paromita looks after her beautiful mother-in-law by applying facial masks, bathing and shampooing each other, going shopping and even ordering a plate of fish fry for her, which Sanaka loves but can no longer eat at home as she is a widow. The two find meaning and their horizons are broadened when they visit the spastic centre with Bablu.

When Paromita and Rajeev get close to each other, Sanaka resents it in telling terms. Perhaps she feels resentment because Paromita is receiving a man's attention, or it could be the fact that after all these years together, she has become extremely possessive about her friend Paromita. Apart from Manimoy, who seems to be her only other friend and who acts like a connection to a past the thoughts of which make her happy, Paromita seems to be her only other confidant.

The strength of their friendship brings Paromita back to nurse Sanaka back at the house which she left when she got married to Rajeev Srivastava. After Paromita's departure, loneliness seems to eat away at Sanaka's very soul, and she seems to while away this state in sorrow. A particular shot of her sitting cross-legged, propped up against the balcony railing, reminds one of Satyajit Ray's *Aparajito* (1956) in which a frail and sick Sarbajaya waits for Apu to come home from Calcutta on a firefly-infested evening. Interestingly, shots from Ray's oeuvre keep interspersing the cinematic world of Aparna Sen. As Sanaka lies suffering, the new daughter-in-law Deepa, Biresh's second wife, comes across as someone who has been unable to penetrate Sanaka's inner world; she also comes across as nothing more than a decorative object in the household.

It is Paromita who is called upon yet again to try and revive a dying Sanaka, and it is Khuku who hits upon this idea. Perhaps in her otherwise skewed world, quarrels, fights, divorces and social ostracization do not exist, and nor do they matter. While the others hesitate to act upon it, Khuku makes the phone call to Paromita with an open mind.

If one studies Sen's film carefully, one notices that it almost reads like a biography of three women in the Sanyal household. While Paromita finds economic empowerment through her job, she nevertheless gets social sanction when Sanaka—afraid of losing her if she divorces Biresh—gives her permission to carry on seeing Rajeev. Paromita, however, escapes, but Khuku and Sanaka are left entrapped in the decrepit old house. Perhaps Khuku also finds escape in her daily ritual of feeding the pigeons on the rooftop and her singing which seems to soar over the neighbouring houses and into the blue sky above. But Sanaka probably finally finds it only in death.

The film comes full circle when Paromita, who stays back until her mother-in-law's shraddha ceremony, feels the baby inside her come alive. Is Sen perhaps trying to say that Sanaka might have found space in her beloved Paromita's life once again—this time as her flesh and blood—her child?

Aparna Sen as Editor

Aparna Sen is one of the best known auteur-actors in Bengali cinema, who, over the years, has emerged as a formidable star presence within the sociocultural milieu of not just West Bengal but also India. Sen started her career as an actor with Satyajit Ray's *Teen Kanya* in 1961, but then became a filmmaker of international repute, though a little late in her career. The persona which Sen has cultivated over the years has been that of a radical, humane, and socially responsible and socially conscious person.

As the editor of an immensely popular Bengali women's magazine, Sen became a cultural commentator through her columns and played an active part, through the magazine, in entering into dialogues with her readers on diverse issues such as communalism and sexuality rights, alongside home remedies and cooking tips.

The women's magazine *Sananda*—launched by the Anandabazar Patrika group in 1986—saw Aparna Sen as one of its first editors from its very inception. There has only been one other editor apart from Sen; however, the magazine reached its zenith with Sen at its helm. She ran the magazine as its editor-in-chief until 2005, making it one of the most popular Bengali magazines in this period. Perhaps one could also call it the Bengali counterpart of *Gladrags*, *Women's Era*, or even *Femina*. However, as Aparna herself said in one of the editorials, *Sananda* was a magazine that even men turned to. It is surprising that in the 1980s, when women would or could turn to *Sananda*, so could men. The topics covered in the magazine would not be gender-specific—something which perhaps aided in the wide circulation of the magazine.

Led by Aparna Sen, *Sananda* set a benchmark as far as quality was concerned. It was a 132-page magazine covering topics as diverse as cooking, travel, fashion, science quizzes, travel writing as well as debates. And if one looks at Aparna's very nifty, tongue-in-cheek, and often humorous editorials, one gets a sense of what she set out to do with *Sananda*.

Through Her Collaborators' Eyes

I spoke to some of Sen's colleagues from that period to gain insight into Aparna Sen, the editor. Surprisingly, all of them insisted on seeing her as a human being rather than focusing on her status as a star. They were more interested in talking about Sen as an editor who proved equal to the task.

The *Sananda* team assisting Sen in various capacities were mostly young men and women who were already working as journalists or were new to the field. Sabarni Das, for instance, says that she began her professional life by assisting Nirmalya Das who was directing a series for Doordarshan Kolkata. Later, she shifted to *Sananda* where she worked for 10 long years: 1998–2008. She would also go on to assist Sen in her first telefilm *Picnic* for Doordarshan in 1991. It is a story about two sisters—played by Shabana Azmi and Farida Jalal—who find themselves confronting each other over their love for the same man.

When asked about her team members at the magazine, Sabarni mentions Vishakha, Sudeshna, Nivedita, Sharbari, Mimi Bhattacharya, Bibi Roy, along with Bibek Das who was a fashion photographer. They were a part of the core team at *Sananda* when the magazine was launched, and it was, of course, led by Aparna herself.

Another key member was Sudeshna Roy. She had been working with *The Telegraph* as a journalist since 1982. But when the opportunity arose for her to begin afresh with *Sananda*, she leapt at the chance. 'I had already worked as a journalist for three and a half years. *Sananda* really changed the way I looked at the world. Aparna Sen taught us to dream.'

Sudeshna was the first among Aparna Sen's associates I spoke with, and the first thing she pointed out was the fact that she found Sen to be an immensely courageous woman who always stood her ground and continues to do so. Roy worked with Sen from 1986 to 1994, and eventually became an associate editor—a coveted post.

Sananda also came to be seen as a trusted friend of women—not only providing them with cooking tips and beauty tips but also carrying political viewpoints for the discerning reader, along with articles on literature as well as a section for film aficionados. The first issue, which was slated to sell 30,000 copies, upended everyone's expectations by selling 75,000 copies instead. Roy says they were given two years to break even, but they managed to do that in six months. *Sananda* proved to be an extremely popular magazine, followed by *Femina*. Ever since then, *Sananda* has been a win-win project for the ABP Group.

Her World, Her Rules

Even a casual glance at the editorials goes on to reveal a lot about their editor. The sheer range of subjects covered in the magazine sheds light on the worldview of the editor and her team. Sudeshna Roy, now a famed film director herself, speaks of her in glowing terms and calls her a very courageous individual.

There were topics covered in *Sananda* which drew a lot of flak from the magazine's readers. Sudeshna particularly remembers an instance when the magazine carried an article on abortion. Victor Banerjee, a well-known Bengali film actor, criticized the move and even threatened to withdraw his subscription to the magazine. He felt that it would be detrimental to families and act as a bad influence on women. This is probably just one random incident, but one gets the feeling that such incidents were probably something Aparna Sen and her team lived with.

Through the 1980s and well into the 90s, a wide range of topics found their way into the readers' hands—diverse topics dealing with abortion, parts of the human anatomy—the eyes, the breast, the body and such others. Sudeshna says with a lot of pride, 'Ours was the first magazine which did food photography.'

The issue of extramarital affairs also found its way into the magazine as a topic. Already, in 1985, Sen dealt with this in her now famous film *Parama*. Roy says excitedly, 'In fact the *Baishnab Padabali* is full of it. It's either unrequited love or extramarital.' While the detractors were many, the magazine managed to make its own place.

As an editor, Aparna Sen proved to be an exemplar. Having made some successful films, Sudeshna says that Sen knew the pulse of the audience. She introduced a section in the magazine in which several of the journalists reviewed films, although as Aniruddha Dhar says, Sen did not like dissecting films, preferring instead to experience them as complete works of art.

Even as an editor, Sen was fulfilling other roles as well; she was also shooting the film *Sati* in a small village near Joka. Sudeshna recalls, 'There was a scene in which a cow was in labour and she was waiting to shoot it. Another scene was a woman giving birth to a girl. Aparna said, "I hope it is a *gabhin* (she calf)." It was and the people were overjoyed and clapped. People started crying when the girl was born. Aparna then went on to say that in nature the female sex is coveted while in the human world it is not.'

Sudeshna says, '*Sananda* really changed the way I looked at the world. I had already worked as a journalist for three and a half years. This was Aparna's first job as an editor, but she dreamt and taught us to dream as well.' Sudeshna recalls that *Sananda* was the first magazine to write about AIDS. The first case as she remembers broke out in Sonagachi (the red-light district in Calcutta) and the woman fled to Madhya Pradesh. When they wrote about it, there were people who began questioning their motives. By 1991, Sudeshna recalls proudly, the government was begging them to write about it in greater detail.

Aparna Sen's humanistic concern for people killed in war, victims of ethnic violence and the degeneration of the environment caused by war found expression not only in her films but also in the editorials she wrote for *Sananda*. Her editorials compulsively and engagingly dealt with social and political issues which were current at that time. Articulating thoughtful opinions and scrupulous post-mortems of sociopolitical realities, the editorials projected a different Aparna Sen, inhabiting a world beyond the comforts of aesthetically furnished living rooms, modular kitchens and upscale saree stores—things which also found a place in *Sananda*. For instance, in several issues following the Babri Masjid riots in December 1992, Aparna Sen relentlessly condemned militant nationalism, vociferously protesting against erecting communal borders in a secular nation. These editorials, in fact, when read now, appear to be preparing the ground for *Mr. and Mrs. Iyer* which she made in 2002.

Sen showed solidarity with her staff when the Babri Masjid was demolished and riots broke out in various parts of the country. Sudeshna notes the harrowing moments and how Sen stayed with the young women at the former's place even though she was a star, while the young men stayed over at the office. This obviously counts towards the idea of Sen possessing a caring and generous nature as well as leadership qualities.

An extensive discussion on the range of topics and people Sen brought in to improve the magazine at every step yielded Bibi Roy's name. Sudeshna says that she had an amazing aesthetic sense when it came to interior decoration and used to help, especially with shooting interiors. Apparently, Sen believed that Bibi was so gifted and had such a heightened sense of aesthetics that she could astound everyone by decorating any place, even with napkins and mere leaves!

'We also made stars out of housewives.' A woman who

loved decorating her house was as important as someone who contributed to her family income with a job. Sen seemed to lay a great deal of emphasis on women being able to manage both the home and their professional lives when the need arose. She herself was a living example of that. She not only brought up her daughters as a single mother, but also contributed much to the world of cinema as a woman film director in India.

A Perfectionist's Touch

Sudeshna Roy offered me a few glimpses of how the magazine was put together; technology not being what it is today, most of the work had to be literally done by hand. Being democratic in her approach, Aparna Sen would ask her team to come up with various topics and ideas. She would tweak them afterwards to suit the magazine's purpose. As Sudeshna puts it poetically, 'She would dream and we would be invited to dream with her.'

Sen, who is known among the film fraternity and her admirers for having an impeccable personal style which borders on the aesthetic, proved influential even at *Sananda* where people tried to emulate her. Both Sabarni Das and Sudeshna Roy said that on several occasions they would get scolded for that and asked to evolve their own styles by Sen.

Sen, who can be called a film director with feminist traits, displayed the same traits as an editor. She wanted to carry a feature on P.T. Usha who, Sudeshna says, was difficult to reach. However, Sen flew down with a photographer and managed to get the story for *Sananda*. Sudeshna says she would come up with topics which would often get shot down by Aparna, but she never gave up. On one occasion, Sen praised her to the others saying, 'Look at Sudeshna, she never shies away from speaking or giving me topics. Even if I scold her, she comes up with five more. Why are you guys so scared of coming up with something?'

Aniruddha Dhar, who had been working with Sen since the second issue of *Sananda*, says that she was an extremely efficient manager of people and had a great bond with her staff. 'She was extremely perceptive and knew exactly who could be entrusted with what kind of work.'

Dhar recalls that Aparna did delegate tasks to others but always retained the final say. She would go over each individual article with care and only when she was satisfied with it would the issue go to press. She was especially meticulous when it came to cover stories.

There used to be a strict deadline which was followed by one and all, and which meant that everything, or at least the final draft of the articles or other pieces, would have to be ready by the 28th of every month. Everybody would be invited to discussions which would include the day-to-day running of the magazine, along with monthly plans, and the goal would be the betterment of the magazine. In four and a half years, there were about 100 issues of the magazine with Sen deciding on the cover story for each issue.

Aniruddha Dhar speaks of the 'brainstorming' sessions which Aparna introduced and during which possible topics for forthcoming issues would be discussed. But usually, it meant camping for three days somewhere far outside Calcutta to ideate, after which they would get back to their routine workload. He says that Sen introduced this idea and it was quite the experience, and it obviously helped in the qualitative output of her staff.

Dhar says that it was an egalitarian world at the *Sananda* office. He would analyse films, with Aparna Sen welcoming all kinds of writings from her staff. 'There was a section that looked at politics,' he says with some pride. 'She had wanted to create another *Desh* magazine.' It is also not surprising given that she has always been interested in sociopolitical issues of the day, which find a place in her films and also in her heart. In 2010, when the Nandigram-Singur issue of land-grabbing by the then government in power in West Bengal flared up, she marched with Mamata Banerjee's party Trinamool Congress because 'it felt right'. Even now, Sen continues to engage with the relevant sociopolitical concerns of the day in her films, which she feels need to be addressed.

Sabarni Das remembers Sen as an editor who insisted that everyone develop the capacity to write on anything. And she developed a journalistic sense of writing which equipped her with the ability to write on topics as diverse as menopause and forensics.

Aparna Sen, says Sabarni, stressed a lot on reading and live interviews. Her motto was to produce good-quality writing. This was something which was also seconded by Aniruddha Dhar when we discussed Aparna Sen, the editor. She encouraged people to do extensive research which she believed would lead to informed and comprehensive coverage of the topic at hand. Reading a few editorials yields surprisingly varied topics—while one issue would look at men's issues, another one would deal with the care of teeth. Sen also required all members of the editorial staff to contribute with write-ups.

The magazine *Sananda* was pioneering in several ways—it was the first coloured magazine and was printed on glossy, high-quality paper, placing it on a par with more renowned women's publications such as *Gladrags* and *Femina*. Dhar explains, 'It was designed to appeal to both types of women—those who were worldly, highly qualified, and well-informed, as well as homemakers. The writing was always serious. Imagine the impact the first issue must have had—Aparna Sen had designed it, and her name featured prominently on the magazine. It has since become inseparably linked with her.'

Later, some of these people who worked with her in *Sananda* went on to assist her in several of her films in various capacities. Sudeshna Roy or Jhumu-di, as she is fondly called by everyone in the Bengali film industry, is a celebrated film director herself. Along with Abhijit Guha, she has made around 24 films till date.

Aniruddha Dhar assisted Sen as associate director in the celebrated *Mr. and Mrs. Iyer* as well as *Paromitar Ek Din*. He continues to write about cinema and has several books to his credit. Having debuted as a costume designer in *Paromitar Ek Din*, Sabarni Das, who found her true calling with that, is working with several leading Bengali filmmakers as costume designer and is quite celebrated for her work now.

And all three of them reaffirm Sen's superior marketing skills. Sudeshna Roy even says that she brought in her sense of cinema to *Sananda*, which obviously contributed a great deal to its success. Sudeshna attributes it to her sense of being able to feel the pulse of the audience, and in this case, of course the readers.

Redefining the Bengali Woman's World

Aparna Sen's editorials were bold, often political, and testified to her strong acumen for understanding the changing society around her. However, it was her perception of ethics and honesty that made her exceptional. She brought the same kind of boldness and courage to her films, and these frequently shook the Bengali middle class out of their complacence.

Her films stand out in terms of sheer content, examining issues such as sexual desires and weaving their narratives around images of war, terrorism and communal violence, and concerns for environmental degradation, one of the biggest banes of modernity—subjects which are not so frequently spoken of at the middle-class dining table. Each of these films constantly returns to the peripheries of society, turning the searchlight on the underprivileged and the marginalized.

Although Sen has never exhibited a deep proletarian consciousness, in her films the underprivileged often take the form of ethnic minorities, ageing people, differently abled individuals, and of course women—still embodying a subalternity within heteropatriarchal structures. This sensitivity to marginalization also found its way into her editorial work. For instance, in *Sananda*, readers were once posed the question: should housewives be paid a salary? The thrust, she explained, was to simplify complex ideas, making them accessible to all. By addressing the concept of valuing domestic labour through the lens of commerce, the magazine extended its focus to include conversations about societal taboos and under-acknowledged work.

Sananda, another important outlet for her thoughts,

had an important role in propelling forward the women's liberation movement in Bengal. The magazine was successful in introducing a new genre of popular literature—combining politics, education and lifestyle issues, it also helped construct the image of the modern 'complete woman'. There was barely anything like this before. It was thanks to *Sananda* that many women were enlightened about 'taboos' (as they were considered by the somewhat conservative elders in my family), such as conjugal issues, divorce, abortion, single motherhood, living together, the cultural significance of sexuality in general, fashion and make-up, interior decoration of 'good taste and high class', and so on.

For homemakers, *Sananda* opened up a whole new world about which, as many readers were quick to note, they were not conscious at all. They got to know a lot about women's liberation, got a new perspective on everyday affairs of the household, and developed a modern vision of life.

The readers of *Sananda* revealed that the one role which this popular magazine definitively and successfully played was in educating both men and women about sexuality and ideas of gender equality. The image of Aparna Sen which emerges from this is that of an editor who is a socialist, humanist artist, and one who would not compromise with her own beliefs. Surprisingly, the picture which emerges is also that of the rich quality of a consumerist magazine which surpassed *Manorama* in terms of popularity. The idea was perhaps to make all-rounders of Bengali women, and needless to say, Sen might even have succeeded in doing so.

Afterword: Towards a More Feminist Politics?

Aparna Sen as a Woman Filmmaker

Since the post-war years when it started to attract greater cultural visibility and critical attention, art cinema has become notorious for pushing the boundaries in 'exploring more sophisticated avenues of women's sensual existence',[22] and being both formally and thematically more daring than Hollywood. This includes a more direct exploration and depiction of sexuality as well as more complex gender identities. The universe of art cinema, however, has been a male-centric one, but with the advent of women directors there are signs of a significant shift. Simone de Beauvoir very acutely remarked that the 'representation of the world...is the work of men', and was, therefore, filtered through 'their own point of view' while at the same time being equated 'with absolute truth'.[23]

However, women directors exploit art cinema's iconoclastic potential to directly address issues of gender

[22]Haskell, Molly, *From Reverence to Rape: Treatment of the Woman in Cinema*, University of Chicago Press, Chicago, 1974.
[23]McCabe, Janet, *Feminist Film Studies: Writing the Woman into Cinema*, Wallflower Press, London, 2005.

identity and its implications, along with offering alternative ways of representing women and questioning already existing representations. One of the foremost names among women art filmmakers is that of Agnès Varda, a prolific director who infused her work with artistic fluidity and freedom of expression. It, therefore, becomes imperative to contextualize Aparna Sen's films within this milieu. Interestingly, both Varda and Sen's films tackle feminist issues, yet they manage to successfully tread the thin line between entertainment and political commitment. One would do well to connect Sen's sensibility in her films with that of one of Varda's most celebrated films, *Cléo from 5 to 7* (1962).

In her second film *Cléo from 5 to 7*, one can see that the representation of the main character Cléo is profoundly distinct from the representations of women curated by male art cinema directors such as Ingmar Bergman, Michaelangelo Antonioni, and to a certain extent, even Luis Buñuel (whose films are a playful take on many issues including even feminism, but not femisnim as we generally understand it; he is a far cry from the other male art film directors I have mentioned). *Cléo from 5 to 7* is a film that deals with the exploration of its woman protagonist's identity—a process set in motion by the horrifying news of her impending death. She has been diagnosed with cancer and the film follows her life during the two hours before she gets the result of her biopsy. As the narrative advances, Cleo gradually transforms from object to bearer of the gaze, which is the first step to regaining her subjectivity and developing as a character. There are a large number of point-of-view (POV) shots, and through continuity editing, Varda shows Cléo as observing the world around her, as well as reverse shots of what she sees. Varda succeeds in addressing feminine stereotypes and surpasses them by presenting the complexity of the woman character.

Another woman filmmaker whose films represent a strong feminist aesthetic is Chantal Akerman. Her widely discussed film *Jeanne Dielman, 23 quai du Commerce, 1080 Bruxelles* (1975) was made at a time when issues of gender representation and their aesthetics were gaining precedence in film scholarship. It is an interesting exploration of the everyday life of a woman who is an ordinary housewife but also a prostitute. What is particularly striking about this film is its lengthy scenes and slow-paced action, which are studiously observed and recorded. In this way, it renders visible a housewife's 'invisible' labour. The housewife/prostitute is de-glamourized, and due to the lack of titillating sex scenes, it dodges any objectification of its protagonist. Although Agnès Varda and Chantal Akerman are big names in the film world, nevertheless their brand of filmmaking was hardly emulated by other women filmmakers. For instance, one cannot find detailed POV shots in any film by Indian women directors. Perhaps this and several other differences are to be expected given the fact that Indian society is a very different world compared to that of either Varda or Akerman. The Indian woman is enmeshed in the patriarchal family, and as such, can afford to have very little time for herself. Also, the woman's life is bound up with that of her family so that a separate existence is inconceivable, as is the idea presented in *Jeanne Dielman*.

Mira Nair, a diasporic filmmaker who made her debut film exactly eight years after Aparna Sen, along with

Deepa Mehta, whose debut film *Fire* (1994) created an uproar in India, made films that specifically dealt with Indian people and the issues directing their lives, depicting Indian women in unconventional and what may even be called controversial ways. Their women are constantly refashioning their identities by rejecting specific behavioural patterns expected from them. They depict Indian women as reclaiming their bodies and sexual identities. Nair constructs Indian women with plural identities and by doing that, she dispels the assumption that Third World women filmmakers are a homogenous entity and that all of them are victims of male oppression.

Deepa Mehta, as I would like to think, is perhaps closer in spirit to Aparna Sen. She is openly critical of society and pointedly challenges hegemonic practices in India through her depiction of its women. She creates resistant narrative spaces for Indian women. For instance, in *Fire*, she uses the domestic sphere to overturn the myth about it being a place to which women are relegated by patriarchy and whose rules they have to obey. It is here that Sita and Radha, her two protagonists, find love and fulfilment in each other. In constructing several different kinds of women characters, Mehta confronts different levels of feminist struggle.

While Nair adopts a more mainstream approach to the construction of her female characters, Mehta can be considered more artistic in her approach. Mira Nair often appropriates the narrative structures of Bollywood and Hollywood in several of her films. Mehta, on the other hand, appropriates specifically Indian nationalist discourses such as history and myth, and weaves them into her cinematic retellings.

The reason I have talked about these two filmmakers is because both began making films around the same time as Aparna Sen, along with the fact that their films and filmmaking interest me. However, the overwhelming question that compelled me to write about them was that of 'Third World' filmmaking challenging convention, which is one of its most important traits. The other important factor is the construction of women characters who explore their sexualities and reclaim their bodies. In their films, they give prominence to Indian women, especially to the diversity of their identities.

Characteristics

In this book, I have tried to look at Aparna Sen's films in a particular way. The thesis was simple—her early films looked at issues that, by and large, dealt with women. Her later films were direct comments on the political scenario unfolding in India. And I have tried to categorize her films as such. This, of course, is a subjective choice and there are many other possible readings of her cinema.

Aparna Sen has always been wary of the term 'feminist', and desists from being called one. Instead, she prefers the term 'humanist'. But no matter which terms she uses to refer to her cinema, there is no mistaking the fact that it largely deals with the world of women. Rituparno Ghosh, whose films are often spoken of in the same breath as Sen's, adopted a different approach altogether. Although his films are also often women-centric, they deal with larger issues such as relationships, rape, sexuality, family, and so on. They do not deal with women's issues in the intimate, sympathetic and empathetic manner in which Sen's films do.

Right from *36 Chowringhee Lane,* Aparna Sen's portrayal of women has been interiorized. It is almost as if one has a window into the soul of the woman. The obsessive way in which the camera follows Miss Violet Stoneham right from the beginning of the film is a good example of this. In fact, one can pick up any of her films at will and put this to test. If one looks at Sanaka in *Paromitar Ek Din*—a film made 20 years after *36 Chowringhee Lane*—it would yield the same result. Although it is named after its protagonist Paromita, the film nevertheless has Sanaka as its focus. It is the budding relationship between daughter-in-law and mother-in-law that becomes important. Even as Paromita enters the Sanyal family with her wedding, the camera, which ought to focus on her life, does not do so. Instead, it focuses a great deal on Sanaka's life and conveys to the audience the claustrophobic quality thereof. This is perhaps to stress the fact that Paromita, in total contrast to Sanaka, would have the guts to walk out of her bad marriage. However, as Sanaka herself reveals, she is no coward either. In fact, she is progressive and courageous, but it is a lack of opportunity that prevents her from trying to begin life anew with her Moni-da.

Even as early as *Parama* (1985), you could see the way the camera ever so obsessively follows the eponymous Parama around. Little details about her life surface while an alternative narration is produced around her husband. A woman's shackled life under patriarchy and her bid to break free are what is uncovered in *Parama*.

In *Yugant* (1995), the primary concern is the breakdown of a marital relationship against the backdrop of environmental concerns. In keeping with the larger issue, Aparna Sen explores very intimate details of a relationship gone awry. She does not judge either Anasuya or Deepak, preferring instead to highlight the highs and the lows of their relationship. It focuses a great deal on Anasuya who feels betrayed by Deepak and is forced to live separately from him. However, she is a career woman and successfully runs a dance academy near Bhubaneswar. What is unusual is that her women characters usually find a way out of their dilemma by either accepting their lot, like Violet Stoneham, or by taking a bold stand like Anasuya and Paromita, who prefer to walk out of their respective marriages rather than compromise, although no one can fault them as wives.

However, some of her women characters are not recognizable in society at all or among women at large. Another peculiarity of her women characters is the fact that they are subjected to ill-treatment and are often willing accessories to their ill-treatment at the hands of men. And when I say this, it covers about 99 per cent of her oeuvre. And one can read it as a sign of malaise in her cinema. The world depicted is a closed one—the woman hedged in by the family, and in most cases, by patriarchy in the guise of the male members of the family, such as a husband or a lover. One is especially reminded of Ingmar Bergman's film *Cries and Whispers* (1972) in this regard, which displays a certain kind of worldview while depicting women. Even Krzysztof Kieślowski's *Red* (1994) from the *Three Colours* trilogy, to a certain extent, depicts his strong dislike of women in the way he depicts Valentine, the protagonist. The other peculiarity exhibited by her films is the fact that most of them do not speak of a context, by which I mean the time and space—neither of which seems to matter much to her.

Gender and Politics

While Aparna Sen's thrust was on gender in her earlier films such as *36 Chowringhee Lane*, *Parama* and *Paromitar Ek Din,* in her later films such as *Ghawre Baire Aaj* and *Arshinahar*, the focus seems to have shifted to politics. In these latter films, Sen's comment on contemporary politics, rather than the human story, seems to drive her narratives forward. Sen is known for her political observations and sometimes her activism, as in the case of the Nandigram and Singur issues.

Sen has always been vocal about sociopolitical issues and she calls herself a 'radical humanist'. Even though one cannot be protesting every little thing that happens in one's country, her protest about the same manifests in her films in a broad way. Very few Indian filmmakers have expressed their political standpoints in the way that Sen has. While this protest may take the form of the depiction of protest marches in her films she mostly chooses to voice it through the exploration of human psychology. While in her earlier films women's issues occupied the centre, one can see that a great change has come over her work—not only in terms of the content but also in terms of her filmmaking—which is direct, more stark, more violent, and definitely more hard-hitting.

Sen can be lauded for the fact that her cinema is sensitive to and about women—something which can't be said about many other women filmmakers. In her films, women occupy the centre stage and it is a woman's world that comes to the fore without getting lost in subplots or myriads of other discourses. Sai Paranjpye, a woman filmmaker, is also a name that is synonymous with Bollywood films that catered to a general audience without displaying any sensibility that's specifically a woman's. In total contrast to this, one can perhaps cite the examples of two films by Shekhar Kapur—*Bandit Queen* (1994) and *Elizabeth* (1998)—which portray their women protagonists in a sensitive manner.

Issues for Exploration

A careful study of Aparna Sen's films yields a sense not so much of patriarchy being criticized as it being a dull noise in all the women's lives. As Sen reiterates in interview after interview, she is trying to make visible the hypocrisy of patriarchy. If one looks at *Parama,* one gets a sense of this. When Parama is found to have transgressed, her oppression is brought into sharp focus. It is at this precise moment that she is found to rebel against all that is old and what was once a part of her very world. Before the family ostracizes her, she willy-nilly puts up with everything including oppression. Nowhere does Sen depict the fact that Parama is in love with Rahul, and it clearly comes across as a physical relationship which gives her succour. In the end, Rahul also turns out to be careless of her feelings when later on he sends the magazine containing her nude picture to her family home. Although one may argue that Rahul is instrumental in aiding her emancipation, nevertheless he comes across as self-absorbed and selfish. What is also surprising is the fact that Sen makes the husband attempt a transgression, perhaps to justify Parama's transgression? In a sense, one can almost read it as an anti-feminist stance. For one, Parama's predicament is not a universal human condition and one finds it difficult to recognize it at all.

Similarly, the ending of another film of hers, *15 Park Avenue,* may very well be read as escapist in nature. Sen's treatment of the subject matter, the theme, and so on falls flat in the face of that ending. Here, Dr Kunal Barua states that Meethi obviously has to be put away in a mental asylum as there is no possible cure for her condition, but then, one wonders why Dr Barua went on meeting Annu and discussing Meethi's case. One could demand a more concrete ending that left one more satisfied. There are works of art with open endings, but even in those, some sense of an ending, or rather, a resolution of sorts, does exist. These are but two particular kinds of gazes—psychological and social—which may be said to be relevant only to individuals and are not universal. Parama's predicament cannot be said to be the lot of every housewife in India.

The Filmmaker's World

Some of the issues which feature prominently in Sen's films are politics, women's issues and female camaraderie, fundamentalism, marginalization, and the failure of heterosexual relationships and unequal friendships. Ritwik Ghatak, Mrinal Sen and Satyajit Ray's films have often been referred to as the forebears of socially conscious and politically heightened cinema. However, filmmakers like Tapan Sinha, Gautam Ghose, Bijoy Bose, Rituparno Ghosh and Aparna Sen churned out films that mirrored a society battling deprivation, glaring gender gaps and human complexities. These films were an expression of resistance from the society on which they were based, and not necessarily from any political movements.

Several of Aparna Sen's films, such as *Arshinagar*, *Mr. and Mrs. Iyer*, and *Ghawre Baire Aaj* are a direct take on politics. Artists react instinctively to the changes around them, which often finds a reflection in their works. These films, she claims, are her reaction to the world around her. While Ray's oeuvre was subtler and more oblique, Aparna's approach is far more direct. So in her last film *Ghawre Baire Aaj*, she takes to the screen to delineate what she calls the 'changing idea of India', and without naming any parties, she hits and hits hard at that. She draws up a villain who is self-centred, self-obsessed and malicious. The film is set in New Delhi, which lends it a certain aura of power-hungriness, and conveys the sense that politics and the need to wield power are inseparable. She also points out the fact that power has the capacity to turn friends into enemies, even prompting them to take lives.

In *Arshinagar*, the focus shifts to the cultural gap and enmity between Hindus and Muslims living in Indian society—a result of the British divide-and-rule policy. Sen adapts *Romeo and Juliet* and states that even in the face of love, such barriers are difficult to overcome. Much of the violence in the film stems from this divide, resulting in the death of the two young protagonists. One can also perhaps see *Arshinagar* as an extension of the theme of *Mr. and Mrs. Iyer*, except that in the latter film, the protagonists are unable to consummate their love. But they do reach an understanding at the end of the journey. The same trope of Hindu-versus-Muslim is played out here, and the journey is symbolic of Meenakshi's growth from a conservative middle-class woman to a human being capable of laying aside traditional orthodox values to help another human being, show love and compassion, and achieve a kind of spiritual growth. The stress is once again on the lack of communal harmony and man's thirst for blood, his intolerance for another and alternative viewpoints, and his inability to embrace the other.

In *Mr. and Mrs. Iyer* as well as *Arshinagar*, the concept of the 'other' becomes quite important. Sen doesn't delve into the question of how the othering takes place, but tries to explore the othered and their relationship with the mainstream. It often ends up being a broad statement on politics, communalism, and so on. The film language she uses in order to express all this is, however, not subtle. In the experimental *Arshinagar*, she uses theatrical devices, loud make-up and costumes which stand out, and plenty of songs, which reflect on the narrative and the plot of the film. In *Mr. and Mrs. Iyer*, the cinematic language employed, although much subtler in tone in comparison to *Arshinagar*, nonetheless uses music to evoke fear, horror, anticipation and love, in turn. The film is shot wonderfully well by Goutam Ghose, a celebrated cinematographer from Bengal, who is able to dexterously capture the light in the shots to beautifully evoke emotions.

In *Ghawre Baire Aaj*, which is a direct political comment on contemporary politics, there are shots of a candlelight march—an important side of the political and social protest in the capital. Sandip's villainy as well as his ideological position are clearly expressed through dialogues. Several shots of Bastar and its inhabitants—the *adivasis*—populate the film and tell us where Sen's sympathy lies. In all, *Ghawre Baire Aaj* embodies a note of loud political protest within her oeuvre, and in it, the subtle treatment of relationships is missing, or rather, glossed over in favour of politics. As is evident from an exploration of her oeuvre, women's issues form the crux of Sen's films. And among these, the disabled 'other' becomes an important point of departure for her kind of cinema.

Another theme which is time and again revisited by Aparna Sen is that of fundamentalism which she says is very close to her heart.[24] And it is something that makes an appearance in several of her films. *Mr. and Mrs. Iyer* is one of her first films which explore this in great detail. It is difficult to say which gains more prominence—the love story or the treatment of fundamentalism within the narrative—as both are deeply enmeshed in each other. The other film which directly deals with it is *Arshinagar*, where the treatment is no longer that subtle. It is in keeping with her changing worldview, which I have noted before, that she is moving from concerns of gender to pressing political issues of the day.

Another important trope is that of the marginalized, and they find a place in her narratives in a big way. While the category of women can also be called marginalized, even within that framework, the category of the disabled other occupies an important place. Even old Miss Stoneham is a marginalized figure because she is from a community that no longer has a place in post-Independence India. The fisherfolk in *Yugant* are also marginalized; they get by on a meagre source of livelihood—fishing—which is fraught with risks. However, they are a simple lot who do not make great demands on life. Parama, who belongs to

---

[24]Personal interview with me.

an upper-class educated Bengali family, also finds herself shunned and marginalized when her transgression is discovered. Her incarceration in a room is symbolic of a bird imprisoned in a cage. Uma, too, is a marginalized figure in *Sati*; she is treated little better than a domestic worker—since she is not only an orphan living as an unwelcome member of her uncle's family but also a deaf and mute woman who is married off to a tree because she is unable to express her desires and wishes. Khuku in *Paromitar Ek Din* is similarly positioned, although she belongs to a middle-class educated family in Calcutta.

In Sen's films, the marginalized are also those people who try to break out of the mould and are rendered lonely in the process. So Meenakshi Iyer, having found love during a bus journey, will remember it for the rest of her life. Similarly, the boy in the wheelchair in the bus, and Cohen, the Jew who betrays his fellow passengers, are all marginalized figures of society. It is fear that drives his world forward. While other films deal with healthy, normal people who belong to mainstream society, Sen's narratives find space for those left behind.

Her films thus come to talk about or represent a pluralistic society, or at least her visions of one. When one looks at her women characters, one gets the sense that Sen is attempting a miracle of sorts—making women capable enough to wrest agency in the face of loss and grief. Not only does she deal with issues that are specific to women, larger questions of economic and social emancipation are also dealt with in her oeuvre. *Goynar Baksho* is an excellent example of this, so is *Parama*. These are films which are tied together by common themes and threads, but at the same time, they succeed in standing on their own as works of art that attempt to make the world a little saner, a little brighter, a little better.

Acknowledgements

Firstly, I wish to thank my mother for helping me conceive the project. She also accompanied me to Aparna Sen's house when I first went to meet her several years ago.

It wouldn't have been possible to do a lot of things in life without my parents' support. Most importantly, thank you both for giving me this writerly life.

I would like to thank: Anindya Chatterjee of Chandrabindoo; Sudeshna Roy, who very kindly agreed to speak with me regarding her stint as journalist and then associate editor at *Sananda*; Sabarni Das, who gave me a detailed interview about her time at the magazine; and Aniruddha Dhar, who, during the course of writing this book, has become 'Aniruddha da'. He encouraged me every step of the way and very kindly looked at some of the chapters for me. Thanks are also due to Satyaki Ghosh who gave me the photo which eventually became the book cover...

Finally, I would like to thank Rohan Datta, senior development editor at Rupa, and Mahasweta for doing such an excellent job with the manuscript. Last but not the least, I would like to thank Yamini Chowdhury at Rupa, who believed in the project and decided to publish it.

Index